AN EXPLOR........ION OF

THE NARRATIVE STRUCTURE

OF

THE KITE RUNNER

MUBASHAR ALTAF

ISBN:
ISBN-13: **978-620-0-23123-9**

THIS BOOK IS PUBLISHED IN 2019, BY
LAP LABMERT ACADEMIC PUBLISHING, MEMBER
OF OMNISCRIPTUM PUBLISHING GROUP 17
MELDRUM STREET BEAU BASSIN 71504,
MAURITIUS

DEDICATION

I dedicate the book to the spirit of my father; Altaf Hussain

CONTENTS

ACKNOWLEDGMENTS

I am very thankful to my teacher Dr. Muhammad Iqbal Butt, who provided me strength and guidance to complete this book. I am also very thankful to the Universe who gave me the chance to do something special.

Chapter 01

Introduction

1.1 Background of the Study

The present thesis deals with a structural analysis of the narrative structure of the text of *The Kite Runner*. It is a Structural exploration of the system of a text. Tyson (2006) states "Structuralism is a human science that tries to understand, in a systematic way, the fundamental structures that underlie all human experience and, therefore, all human behavior and production" (p. 209). The researcher seeks to understand literature as an aesthetic human product. The researcher applies the theory of five codes stated by Roland Barthes in his seminal work, *S/Z*. The present research explores the following five codes working behind the narrative of *The Kite Runner*; (i.e., Proairetic code, Hermeneutic code, Semantic code, symbolic code, and Cultural code). In the novel, the researcher's part is to find binary opposition and explore their role in the determination of meanings. In the novel, *The Kite Runner*, the researcher emphasizes different kinds of binaries which include: geographical, emotional, relational, religious, seasonal, and verbal. As for as meaning the text is concerned, it offers five voices for analysis, no single concrete meaning is found. It is text having multi-meanings.

1.2 Introduction of Author and Text

Khaled Hosseini is an Afghan Author who was born on 4 March 1965 in Kabul. *The Kite Runner* and *Thousand Splendid Suns* are best sellers on an international level, publish in 34 countries. *The Mountain Echoed* is his recent novel. He lives in northern California. He has done M.D from the University of California. He is a practicing doctor and part-time writer. *The Kite Runner* was his first novel published in 2003. The story is set in Afghanistan and around the two boys Hassan and Amir. *The Kite Runner* has received the South African Bookie Prize in 2004.

By writing this novel, *The Kite Runner*, Hosseini has become one of the bestseller novelists of the world. Hosseini writes this novel to make the world realize the struggles of his Afghan people against violent forces. Paying just tribute to his present work in *New York Time*, it is written: "Khaled Hosseini gives us a vivid and engaging story that reminds us how long his people have been struggling to triumph over the forces of violence-forces that continue to threaten them even today" (ibid blurb).

The novel *The Kite Runner* is written in 2003. It takes place in Afghanistan and America The story is about Amir and Hassan. They two are friends and has a relation of master and servant. In the start of the novel, they both are happy and enjoy their life with the company of one another. But with the passage of time, their relationship becomes fade. Amir starts to ignore Hassan as he is raped by their opposite group of children. Amir remains silent on this brutal incident and ignores Hassan. He tries his level best to get Hassan out from his house. He accuses Hassan although he knows that Hassan is not wrong. Amir's behavior creates suspense in the mind of his father. His father does not agree to his demand. But Hassan and his father Ali leave the house. Baba and Amir escape to America. After many years In America Amir receives a call from Afghanistan from the friend of his father. His past calls him back for salvation. He comes to know that Hassan has died and his son is in the hands of the Taliban. In the novel, Hossein tries to show the brutality by the Taliban on Afghans. Amir goes back to Afghanistan for salvation and to bring Sohrabout from the groups of Terrorists. He goes on a journey of solace. He is revealed by many harsh truths in Afghanistan. He tries his level best to help Sohrab to succeed in his mission. He brings Sohrab with him in America. Amir finds his salvation in his friendship, in the son of Hassan.

1.3 The Theorist for The Study

The researcher takes Roland Barthes as a theorist for the present thesis. Barthes was one of the famous theorists of France, in the 1960s. He challenges the orthodox practice of literary criticism and founded an unconventional form of criticism. He is inspired by the work of Ferdinand de Saussure and Sigmund Freud. He defines literature as "a message of the signification of things and not their meaning (by signification I refer to the process which produces the meaning and not this meaning itself)" (Barthes 1972, p.263). He stresses the process of signification. According to him, Language is not a natural phenomenon rather it is a system. It is only a system of references. If we limit the language to being a natural medium for a reader to seize the meaning, it is as if we are limiting a signifier to just one signified and repressing all discourses into one meaning, which is not possible.

In *Elements of Semiology* (1967), he believed that all the sign-system of human culture can be explained by the structuralist method, but how can we explain this structuralist discourse? We have a first-order discourse that is the language of the subject and we have a 'second-order' discourse that is the language of the semiological investigator. This second-order discourse is also called metalanguage. We can find an infinite regress, which abolishes the authority of all metalanguages. In this sense, all discourses are equally fabricated and none stand apart in the place of truth, In other words, we do not have a single truth (Truth), but a number of truths and each of them is capable of creating its own fictive reality (cf. Barthes 1973).

In his seminal essay, *The Death of the Author*, he appears as a poststructuralist. Structuralism treats individual utterances or paroles as the product of impersonal systems, langue. What is new in Barthes is the idea that readers are free to open and close the text's signifying process without respect for the signified. There is no Meta signified that limit the reader's interpretation, rather a number of signifieds, as many as the reader wants.

1.4 Roland Barthes' *S/Z*

Barthes' *S/Z* (1970) is a structuralist work. like structuralists, Barthes is looking for a single structure to see all the world's stories in. Each text refers back to the infinite sea of the "already written". He introduces two concepts: "readerly' (*lisible*) text and 'writerly" (*scriptable*) text. A readerly text lets the reader to be a passive consumer of fixed meaning and sees referentiality as the primary function of language. According to Paul de Man in his essay, *Resistance to Theory* (1986), "By linguistic terminology it is meant a terminology that designates reference prior to designating a referent and takes into account, in the consideration of the world, the referential function of language or, to be somewhat more specific, the considers reference as a function of language and not necessarily as an intuition" (de Man 1986, p. 8). The readerly text does the opposite of what de Man said. It considers reference as intuition. Writerly text, on the other hand, does exactly the same as de Man said. It turns a reader into an active *producer* of the text and allows the 'I' which is "already itself a plurality of other texts" to have a significant role in the production of the text. This will result in the plurality of the text. The plurality that has different degrees and should not be reduced by any privileged interpretation. The writerly text exists only in theory, as Barthes says, "this ideal text is a galaxy of signifiers, not a structure of signifieds; it has no beginning . . . we gain access to it by several entrances, none of which can be authoritatively declared to be the main one; the codes it mobilizes extend as far as the eye can reach" What are these codes? The notions that are presented in this section are highly related to reader-response theory, in which readers complete the work's meaning through interpretation, and we can say that we have as many interpretations as the readers want. In poststructuralism, although this idea is valued there are some limits to the interpretations of the readers which can be appreciated by the logic of the work. Barthes expresses these limitations through five codes, that create a network, but codes do not have a clear structure, they are rather virtually infinite 'voices' of the text that each of them for a while may dominate the text. This concept of having different voices that are equally developed within the text reminds one of Mikhail Bakhtin's concept: the idea of "polyphony" in novels that were inspired by Dostoevsky's works. In *The Brothers Karamazov*, for instance, Dostoevsky developed many voices, among them the voices of three brothers (Dmitri, Ivan, and Alyosha), that equally contribute to the process of the story. The five voices that Barthes has introduced, are doing the same thing as the voices in *The Brothers Karamazov*, and that is developing a set of incomplete meanings that allows the reader freedom of choice and the duty of completing them, in a way that they like.

1.5 Codes or Voices

Roland Barthes analyzes Sarrasine in his seminal work, *S/Z*. Barthes divides the text into fragments, lexias, reading units to apply five codes, which are five voices

1. Proairetic code (ACT)

2. Hermeneutic code (HER)

3. Semic code (SEM)

4. Symbolic code (SYM)

5. Cultural code (REF)

The hermeneutic code (HER) or the voice of truth, refers to any element in a story that raises questions and, therefore, exists as a puzzle for the reader and creates suspense for him/her that he/she wants to know the answer to them. This enigma moves the narrative forward, but it does not just reveal the answer to these questions. The narrative tries to postpone reaching to the answers as long as it can by the use of elements such as snares (thoughtful avoidances of the truth), equivocations (mixtures of actuality and snare), partial answers, suspended answers, and jammings (acknowledgments of insolubility). As Barthes explains, "The variety of these terms (their inventive range) attests to the considerable labor the discourse must accomplish if it hopes to *arrest* the enigma, to keep it open" (Barthes 1990: 76). This code moves from questions to answers and is irreversible because once a secret is revealed, it cannot be unrevealed. In *Sarrasine* the enigma surrounds La Zambinella. the question arises 'Who is she?' which is finally revealed ('she' is a castrato robed as a woman), there come so many delays in the process that of reaching the answer.

A theory which is going to be applied has been taken from Roland Barthes' book *S/Z*. Roland Gerard Barthes was a cultural theorist and semiotician. Barthes was born on 12 Nov. 1915. He was a very influential writer who affected not only structuralism and Semiotics but also Post-Structuralism, social and cultural theory. His most important book is *S/Z* in which he presents a detailed analysis of the story *Sarrasine* written by Balzac. The idea of Five Codes is also explored in that book.

By propagating this theory, Barthes claims that every story contains the Five Codes (i.e. Symbolic code, Hermeneutic code, Proairetic code, Semantic code, and Referential code). In the current research, the researcher applies all Five Codes one by one.

In Barthes' view of identifying a word, an entity or thought, it is necessary to study its opposite word, entity or thought. In order to support Barthes' concept of symbolic code second theory which is going to be applied has been taken from Levis Straus' model of Binary Oppositions. Claude Levis Straus was born in 1908 and died in 2009. He was social structuralist. He argues society depends on the structure which is definitely based on Binary Oppositions.

Barthes's five-fold codes include Hermeneutic, Semantics, Symbolic, Proairetic and Cultural codes. The Hermeneutic code is proposed as all those units whose function is to articulate in various ways of questions, their responses and the variety of chance events which can either formulate the question or delay its answer or even constitute an enigma and lead to its solution. The Proairetic code manifests in tonal-moral, collective, unnamed and mighty form. The cultural code is the chamber of referring the text out there to the public knowledge. This code comes with the scope of mythology and ideology. The Cultural code manifests as tonal "moral", collective, unnamed and mighty form which represents what is called "wisdom".

The Semantics code or signifiers is defined as connotative meaning which employs significations and produced by specific signifiers. The symbolic codes of the poems will be analyzed in the present study." The Symbolic code embraces identifiable structures which are repeated regularly in different forms and modes through the text and eventually makes the dominant structure "(Barthes 1974, Sojoodi, 2011, 148-150).

It is not sometimes easy to identify symbolic and semantics codes because they are highly interconnected. Barthes believed that each piece is a sagacious sign and has an independent life. Speech is created through their combination which is started from the life inside each piece (Barthes1990, Ahmadi, 2014, 212).

- The theory has been taken from Roland Barthes' book *S/Z*.

- Roland Gerard Barthes was a cultural theorist and semiotician. Barthes was born on 12 Nov. 1915.

- He was a very influential writer who affected not only structuralism and Semiotics but also Post-Structuralism, social and cultural theory.

- His most important book is *S/Z* in which he presents a detailed analysis of the text of the novel "Sarrasine" written by Balzac. The idea of Five Codes is explored in that book.

- By propagating this theory, Barthes claims that every story contains the Five Codes (i.e. symbolic code, hermeneutic code, Proairetic code, semantic code, and cultural code).

- The Hermeneutic code is proposed as "all those units whose function is to articulate in various ways of questions, their responses and the variety of chance events which can either formulate the question or delay its answer or even constitute an enigma and lead to its solution".

- The Cultural code manifests as moral tone, collective, unnamed and mighty form which represents what is called "wisdom".

- The Semantics code or signifiers are defined as connotative meaning which employs significations and produced by specific signifiers. (the voice of the author)

- The Symbolic code embraces identifiable structures which are repeated regularly in different forms and modes through the text and eventually makes the dominant structure. (binaries in the text)

To conduct the study, textual evidence is collected to explore and analyze the significance of binary opposition and symbolic code in the text of the novel. This research is qualitative in its nature. For the analysis of the text, the guiding principles have been taken from Roland Barthes' theory of *Five Codes*. In order to support Barthes' concept of symbolic code second theory which is going to be applied has been taken from Levis Straus' model of Binary Oppositions. Claude Levis Straus was born in 1908 and died in 2009. He was social structuralist. He argues society depends on the structure which is definitely based on Binary Oppositions.

The present study is exploratory research. One text has been selected for detailed analysis. According to data, it is qualitative in nature. To conduct the study, textual evidence is collected to explore the five codes working underlying the narrative of *The Kite Runner*. This research is deductive and fundamental since it deals with theoretical understanding. For the analysis of the text, the guiding principles have been taken from Roland Barthes' theory of *Five Codes*. The researcher divides the analysis into five subparts. The narrative will be analyzed from five dimensions. The study does not follow a straight line of analysis rather it follows a multi-layered, process that continually builds upon itself until a meaningful and verifiable explanation is attained. In short, it is exploratory, descriptive, research. Deductive reasoning has been applied. It is qualitative research.

Many studies have been conducted on Khaled Hosseini's writings and especially on his novel, *The Kite Runner* around the world. Dian Ratna Pertiwi, a researcher, in her paper, *"Ethnicity in Khaled Hosseini's novels (The Kite Runner, A Thousand Splendid Suns, and The Mountain Echoed): A Sociological Approach"*, studies ethnic identity in ethnicity, in Afghanistan. Vaishali, in his research, *"Representation of Afghanistan Cultural Identity in Khaled Hosseini's The Kite Runner"*, finds that Afghanistan is the land of various ethnic groups. So that there are many different cultures and all groups call proudly themselves Afghans. Anjitha Gopi researches the violence, bloodshed, and decadence of Afghanistan in the paper, *"Resurrecting Afghanistan: Khaled Hosseini's The Kite Runner"*. As Anjitha argues that "Afghanistan, over the past few decades, has had various understandings and connotations attached to it and sadly, everything narrows down to violence, bloodshed, and terrorism (Gopi, 2017)." Rashid Mahmood and Syed Kazim Shah, in their collective work *"The Role of Linguistic Devices in Representing Ethnicity in The Kite Runner",* investigates the role of linguistic devices which writer has used for representing ethnicity in the novel *"The Kite Runner".* They proliferate that "the results of the research reveal that the writer has employed linguistic manipulation as a powerful instrument to represent ethnicity. He has used specific linguistic devices, like foregrounding, backgrounding, presupposition, omission, framing and first-person narrative, to influence the readers to make them accept the ideological message contained in the text. This study will help in developing critical thinking of the readers by enabling them to decode text manipulation (Mahmood and Kazim, 2013)." Imtiyaz Ahmad Tantray lifts his pen on the violence against women in Afghanistan represented in the novel *"The Kite Runner".* In his paper, *"Living on the Edge: Women in Khalid Hosseini's Novel, The Kite Runner".* Ahmad explores "how during a critical phase in Afghanistan's history, the conditions of violence and conflict magnified the oppression of its women (Ahmad, 2017)."

There has been a research gap of exploration of the narrative structure of the text of Khalid Hosseini. In order to fill the gap and participate in the process of critical analysis of the Asian text from the structural point of view, the researcher analyzes and explores the narrative of *The Kite Runner*. the researcher takes the theory of five codes proposed by Roland Barthes in his famous work *S/Z*.

1.6 Thesis Statement

"The narrative is not a random assemblage of events, rather it has a structure. Understanding one text gives us an understanding of all narratives. A narrative shares a common structure with other narratives, which can be analyzed. Any text is, in fact, marked by the multiple meanings suggested by the five codes" (Roland Barthes, *Introduction to the Structural Analysis of the Narrative*).

1.7 Research Questions

1. How do the binary oppositions play a pivotal role in constructing the meaning of the narrative of *The Kite Runner*?

2. What are the elements of narrative which create tension in the plot?

3. How do enigmatic elements play an important role in the formation of the narrative of *The Kite Runner?*

4. What are the elements in the narrative which signify Semantic code in *The Kite Runner?*

5. How do different elements; social, cultural, linguistic, historical and aesthetic, interact for artistic work (*The Kite Runner)* to be realized?

1.8 Research Objectives

The main objective is to explore the Five Codes (Proairetic, Hermeneutic, semantic, symbolic and cultural code) working underlying the text of *The Kite Runner*

To find out the relation of Meanings of the text and binaries in *The Kite Runner.*

Another objective is to discover the voice of culture (historical, social, political, and literary references) in the text.

To explore the elements and signs which have the connotative meaning which represents the voice of the author in the text?

To discover the Puzzling and enigmatic elements which have played a central role in the creation of the narrative of *The Kite Runner*.

1.9 Significance of the Study

It gives an understanding that literary creations are aesthetic products whose purpose is to give aesthetic pleasure to the readers. It has nothing to do with politics, history, philosophy or religion. It makes us a better teacher of a literary text. This study enhances our understanding of the literary text. According to the Barthes, there are many genres of the literary text, but all have the same underlying structure. So understanding a network of the text provides us with insight about all literary texts. So it is a contribution in the field of narratology. It highlights the cognitive process in which the readers perceive the meanings of the text by binaries. So it touches psycholinguistics from one hand and semantics from the other hand.

Barthes took the linguistics concepts of Ferdinand Saussure and applies to the different text in order to analyze structurally. He was structuralist who seeks a code, a universal structure behind every text. His famous work *S/Z* shows his keen interest in structures. There he devised the concept of Five codes and then presents a detailed analysis of the Sarrasine by Balzac. That analysis provides us with an insight into the universal structure of every literary text. The researcher takes the theory of five codes of Barthes and applies to the text of *The Kite Runner*. The researcher explores the underlying structure of the text and finds that all five codes are working behind the narrative. According to the Barthesian terms, *The Kite Runner* is a writely text. The researcher applies all five codes one by one and explores the text. it has a hermeneutic thread, it has suspense and beautiful plot construction. It contains social, historical, political and cultural references. This research article also aims at an understanding of the role of binary opposition in the determination of meanings. In the novel, *The Kite Runner*, the researcher emphasizes six kinds of binaries which include: geographical, emotional, relational, religious, seasonal, and verbal. Roland Barthes propounds the idea of Symbolic Code in his book *S/Z*. Barthes introduces symbolic code which refers to the antithetic code. In Barthes' view of identifying a word, an entity or thought, it is necessary to study its opposite word. One sign is recognized by its opposite sign. Straus claims that the human brain is language structured and language is a binary system. He argues just as words are based on contrast, human thoughts are also based on contrast to derive meanings. The findings of this research suggest that the structure of Hosseini's novel *The Kite Runner* is constructed out of binaries and dialectic codes. In conclusion, we can say all codes play their vital part in the creation of an artistic product (*The Kite Runner*). The researcher applies all five codes and explores the text from five dimensions. It has a hermeneutic thread, it has suspense and beautiful plot construction. It contains social, historical, political and cultural references. This research also aims at an understanding of the role of binary opposition in the determination of meanings. In the novel, *The Kite Runner*, the researcher emphasizes four kinds of binaries which include: geographical, emotional, relational, religious, seasonal, and thematic. According to the Barthesian terms, we can say that the kite runner is a lisible (readerly) text. *The Kite Runner* is a well constructed aesthetic product which gives pleasure to the readers.

Chapter 02

Literature Review

To conduct a literature review, The researcher has taken around twenty research works related to the selected text, *The Kite Runner*, theoretical framework and the author Khaled Hosseini. The strategy of least important to most important has been adopted. After a brief review of all selected researcher works the researcher finds the gap of research.

The title of the first research paper is *"Racial Discrimination Towards The Hazaras As Reflected In Khaled Hosseini's The Kite Runner"*. In the research paper, the researcher explored the tribal skirmish among the Hazaras and Pashtuns, two unlike ethnic plus races in Afghanistan. Fadlallah Satya Handayani, then the researcher finds out the causes of regarding ethnic discernment in order to evaluate its impacts. This study uses the theories concerning racial discrimination plus racism, psychological approach, and the sociological approach. It is concluded that racial discernment is injurious to the societies for it instills people to create decisions concerning others in relation to group-based prospects or else criteria. The title of the next research paper is *"Neo-colonialism in Afghanistan as a representation of America in Khaled Hosseini's novel The Kite Runner"* written by Sri Utari. The researcher emphasizes to know neo-colonialism in Afghanistan that how the neo-colonialism done by Pashtun ethnic is said to be the neo-colonialism of the United State of America. He uses content analysis. The analysis involves a qualitative method to interpret and report descriptively. All data is analyzed and categorized according to sociological theory especially symbolism theory which disrupts symbols to uncover the cultural meaning. The researcher highlights the colonialism of the United States of America in Afghanistan. Next research paper is written by Nina Farlina. The title of this research paper is *"The Issue of cultural identity in Khaled Hosseini's The Kite Runner".* The researcher throws light on cultural Identity as well as character analysis by using a qualitative descriptive method in order to describe two central characters, Amir and Hassan who belong to the same community but represent diverse ethnic and religious groups.

This researcher includes next paper about *"Child Abuse In Khalid Hosseini's The Kite Runner".* It is written by Fatimat uz, Zahra khoirun Nisa. In this paper, the issue of child abuse is analyzed. It deals with the concept that literature reflects life depicting child abuse. The research categorizes literary criticism under the curtain of social psychological approach in order to show social phenomena occurring among characters. The problem of child abuse, in society, is associated with social psychology.

Next work which is taken by the researcher for review is a thesis entitled as *"Amir's Anxiety and Motive in Khaled Hosseini's The Kite Runner".* It is written by Ajeng Pancar Tamara. The researcher analyzes Amir's anxiety and motive. The use of psychological and structural tactics is made to scrutinize the extrinsic and intrinsic components. The first one helps to examine motives (safety plus security needs, love as well as belonging needs, then self-confidence needs), neurotic, realistic, and moral anxiety practiced by Amir. The second method is used to study the clash of setting, characters, and plot.

Next research work for the review is also psychological. The topic is " *Thematic Study Of Khaled Hosseini's novel The Kite Runner"*. It is written by Waseem Ahmad. The researcher explores betrayal, guilt, redemption, and salvation. The novel depicts a voyage of self-discovery by acknowledging Amir's past experiences. It discloses his journey from babyhood to adulthood, from unfaithfulness to redemption. It displays his return to the motherland after being blemished and ragged by war. Besides, the instability of a Taliban led regime reveals his expedition toward redemption and self-identity.

Next, The researcher takes Hiqma Nur Agustina's article is entitled as *The Kite Runner: My Passion of Literature.* The researcher analyzes the brotherhood reality and the discriminative treatment among the people because of different ethnic identity by using the qualitative descriptive technique. He shows a sense of brotherhood among Amir, Hassan which further reflects brotherhood in Afghan's social set up even, in the conflicting epoch. Amir's life influenced by Hassan not only in his adulthood living in Afghanistan but also when he is matured living as a migrant in American soil.

Next researcher work is not a psychological study but linguistic study. The research work is " *The Levels Of Power Relationship In The Kite Runner*". It is written by Malik plus Murtaza. The researcher uses critical discourse analysis to analyze the linguistic manipulation using Huckin's analytic tools of CDA in order to decode the text manipulation for making readers receive ideological meaning enclosed in the script. It unfolds commanding relations, domination, subjugation, despotism, and downgrading in the novel.

The next research article is about *"The Kite Runner: Role Of Multicultural Fiction In Fostering Cultural Competence"*. It is written by Dr. Tarana Parveen. The researcher explores the role of multicultural literature to promote cultural awareness. The researcher depicts Afghan Culture which brands it a dominant device affecting racial indulgent. It helps to break stereotypes and falsifications made by the media. Besides, it bargains a prospect to contemplate about humanity behindhand hysterical media.

Next work for review is taken is a research paper is *"The Role of Linguistic Devices in Representing Ethnicity in The Kite Runner"*, Syed Kazim Shah, Malik, plus Mahmood are authors of this paper. The researcher analyses the role of the linguistic devices used to epitomize society in the text. The researchers have used explicit linguistic strategies such as presupposition, foregrounding, omission, backgrounding, framing besides the first-person narrative to make readers accept ideological dispatch confined in the novel.

The next research paper is about the Literatury Portrayal of Novel *The Kite Runner* By Khaled Hosseini. This research paper is written by three authors Sulekha Sundaresan, Dr.K.Sumathi and Dr.P.Kolappadhas. The researcher portrays the fellowship reality. He demonstrates that true fellowship is strong in association amid Amir and Hassan, then between Amir and Sohrab. This impressions clan association in Afghan humanity even in the age of disputes. The growth of personality regarding numerous tribes strengthens discriminative dealings amongst the common populace.

The title of the next thesis is *"Colonial Invasion And Inner Conflicts Of Afghanistan In Khaled Hosseini's The Kite Runner And A Thousand Splendid Suns"* presented by Shahil Mon P P. The researcher explores a close look at the difficulties of life in Afghanistan and investigates the treatment of history, especially that of inner conflicts and invasions of colonial powers which made the land, the land of unending terror.

The following research paper is titled as *"Image of Islam in Postcolonial Novels: E. M. Forster's A Passage to India and Khaled Hosseini's The Kite Runner"* written by Bahman Jabar Mohammed. In this paper, the researcher portrays the image of Muslims to show how Islam and Muslims are framed and stereotyped before and after the September 11 attacks. They apply Homi K. Bhabha's cultural theory and Edward Said's Orientalism to pinpoint and ascertain the narratives forming and shaping the texts. Furthermore, special attention is directed to the representations of Islam and Muslims and what stereotypical images constructed and attributed to them in both novels.

The researcher takes Robin Jocius' research paper is entitled *"Exploring Adolescents' Multimodal Responses to The Kite Runner: Understanding How Students Use Digital Media for Academic Purposes"*. The researcher uses a multimodal analysis framework. He discovers the following questions. It comprises how pupils' multimodal retellings are coupled with fictitious policies interceded in the text. Moreover, it depicts how the choice of compositional tools and different modes are composed within the novel. The findings of the study are helpful to shape adolescents' multimodal configuration rehearses in the educational domain.

The title of the next research paper is *"Analysis of Hassan's Tragedy in the Kite Runner from the Three-dimensional Ethical Perspective"* by Peng Yuan-yuan. The researcher depicts three-dimensional principled standpoints. Hassan's tragedy is greatly correlated with countrywide and religious integrities. It is also prejudiced by distorted family morals.

The next set of research works are related to the theory selected by the researcher. The following papers apply Roland Barthes concepts for critical analysis. The first research paper which is chosen by the researcher for the review is *"Visually communicating 'honesty': A semiotic analysis of Dorset Cereals' packaging"*. It is presented by Jessica Burrows, who Uses the semiotic analysis for the research. This study examines Dorset Cereals' visual communications regarding brand beliefs of honesty through wrapping design. This relates the works by Barthes, Williamson, plus Saussure, for exploring Cereals' use of widely-held consumer principles as well as pre-existing systems of meanings in order to paradigm its apparition of honesty.

The Title of the next research paper is *"Analysis of the Binary Oppositions of Django Unchained"* is presented by Yu Chunmei. This paper analyzes binary oppositions in the film using a structuralistic perspective. It not only tries to search its profound fundamental structure but also unfolds the communal connotation to the spectators. This learning bids an altered viewpoint of obligation for the movie.

The researcher takes the next Research paper which is written by Fatemeh Shahpoori Arani titled as *"The Play of Codes and Systems in Pygmalion: Bernard Shaw and Roland Barthes"*. The researcher has applied "the linguistic idea of the critical period hypothesis." This editorial scrutinizes relationship among education, cultural codes, and the issues of communal flexibility in a snobbish society of Pygmalion. Pygmalion can be taken as demonstrating that cultures are made by codes, not by nature. This can be qualified besides learned. Shaw suggests the possibility of coach lower class people by using higher-class ethnic codes. Moreover, he validates that culture is time-bound. The borders amid lower and elite-class traditional codes are going to fade at the time making it tough to differentiate real upper-class agents from fake ones.

The next article is written by F. Soltani titled *"An Analysis of Sheikh Sanaan's Story Based on Roland Barthes's Theory of Codes"*. The researcher has applied Roland Barthes's Theory of

Codes. This paper investigates the story with the viewpoint of five codes depicted by Barthes. These codes are concerned with meanings, and Culture. Using these five codes, the research analyzes the story of Sheik Sanaan in order to indicate the analysis of diverse types of narratives by using precise rules and doctrines.

The following article is written by Muhammad Saleem titled as *"Investigating Hemingway's Cat in the Rain within the Framework of Barthesian Codes"*. He applied the Barthesian theory of codes. This paper explores Hemingway's short narrative *"Cat in the Rain"* in the light of poststructural narratology. This approach precedes Derrida's deconstruction which claims that different social, cultural and aesthetic factors take part in the actualization of artistic creation. Besides, the critical exploration of each of its building block is essential for grasping the worth and implication of the aestheticized product. This process of art's deconstruction contains an investigation of Proairetic, hermeneutic, semic, symbolic and racial codes. Rationalizing and justifying this, the researcher chooses the next article which is written by Seyed AliBooryazadeh. He gave its title as *"Barthes' Irreversible Codes:*

An Intertextual Reading of James Joyce's, Araby". The researcher has applied the Barthesian theory of five codes. According to Barthes semiology studies how language personifies the world. In the structural investigation of Balzac's *"Sarrasine"* in *S/Z,* he explains five types and roles of these codes. Proairetic code, basic narrative actions, Hermeneutic code, narrative turning points, Cultural code prior social knowledge, Semic code medium-related codes, and Symbolic code, themes. This research elucidates that *Araby* thrives with two of these irreparable codes named as proairetic then hermeneutic.

The next research paper is written by Chabha Ben Ali Amer titled as *"Death of the Author and Birth of the Reader in Thomas Hardy's Jude the Obscure".* This study is conducted to introduce the concept of the Death of the Author developed by the French theorist Roland Barthes, and to propose a model applied to Hardy's Jude the Obscure according to the Barthian Reading of a text. this paper will discuss Barthes' approach to analyze a literary text, which is considered as a reading technique employed to deduce specific meanings lying beneath the deep structure of the anonymous sentences in a piece of writing, disregarding the authorial background. Therefore, the reader's intention becomes the focus of our investigation. Accordingly, we are required to yield to the five codes and the lexical analysis proposed by Barthes in *S/Z* in order to exclude the constant reference to the Author and to enhance it with the Reader-Response Theory.

The next work is a thesis. The thesis is written by Sarah Haybittle titled as *"Correspondence, trace and the landscape of narrative: a visual, verbal and literary dialects"..* Gerard Genette's Narrative Discourse and Roland Barthes' *S/Z* deliver a theoretical framework for this. This research analyzes the foundational material (the letters). It studies the impact of literary codes on visual methods and configurations. Gennette and Barthes' theories are applied to examine from two dimensions. The visual text is probed through codes and transfer of meanings are analyzed.

The researcher selects the next research work on translation studies, where Roland Barthes theory has been applied for analysis. This article is written by "Paweł Jureczek" titled as

"Literary Translation Quality Assessment: An Approach Based on Roland Barthes' Five Literary Codes". This article is dealt with the theory of "Barthesian theory of five codes". Its basic framework is connected with J. House's description of translation, which proceeds both micro as well as macro constructions. It uses Barthes's theory of five codes to interpretation, E Dolet's five principles to analyze, Tytler's three ideologies for the translator, then Belloc's six general instructions for translating a prose text. Rodriguez's and House's findings on literary translations are used as a base for additional growth.

The next article is about narrative interpretation. This article is written by Vered Tohar titled as *"An Alternative Approach for Personal Narrative Interpretation: The Semiotics of Roland Barthes"*. In this paper, the author proposes Roland Barthes's analytical method appeared in *S/Z* as a novel technique of scrutinizing personal stories. The five codes labeled in the book are related to domains of poetics, linguistic, and culture. It exposes facets that are entrenched in the deep erection of narratives. These codes reveal the development of the professional careers of teacher educators.

The next chosen research paper is written by Asa Henriksson titled as *"The Reader Strikes Back: A Narratological Approach to Paul Auster's The New York Trilogy"*. In this article, the researcher has used narratology provided by Roland Barthes in *S/Z* to investigate Auster's text. The researcher would show that it is by using the five codes that Barthes presents in *S/Z*, that the researcher is able to display how Auster challenges the conventions. In this reading researcher would also relate The New York Trilogy to other detective fiction and to Barthes' notion of 'the death of the author'.

Following research, the article is written by Bangkalan. The article is about a story of 'Gus jakfar' and Barthesian theory influences in the development of plot construction of theory. Roland Barthes, while analyzing Balzac's story *Sarrasine* has identified five codes. These codes describe a network that forms a space of meaning in the text. The present research uses Barthes five codes to analyze the short story of 'Gus Jakfar' by K.H.

Musthofa Bisrito in order to perceive how far the theory is valid in a different social and ethnic setting.

The Researcher has selected the next researcher work which is a thesis. This thesis is written by Sandra Ohse Fredriksen titled *"Roland Barthes's Ancient rhetoric: A translation"*. Basically, this work is about the translation of Ronald Barthes. Syntagmatic and paradigmatic is applied to study this work. The principles of Saussurean linguistics, Barthes divides his work into two main sections, a syntagmatic section, and a paradigmatic section. The first deals with the origins of rhetoric as it was used in courts of law to try property cases and introduces the reader to the works of Aristotle, Cicero, Quintilian, etc. It traces the various turns of classical rhetoric through the Middle Ages and into the modern era, with special attention to pedagogical methods and trends. The next work for a literature review is a research article which is written by Zahra Joharchi titled as *"The Simurgh Myth in Shahnameh According to Barthes's Five Main Codes"*. In this article, the researcher has applied Barthes's five main codes to analyze the given text mentioned above in the topic. sign in mythology but as a secondary semiotic system as it is composed of semiotic chains which came into existence before it. We meet two languages in mythology first, the language that myth is established by and second the meta-language that defines the first language. Myth changes history in nature and it is a speech figured to be right. The feature of the myth is changing meaning into form. Language is the author's tool and the text they create analytically different from others. The text is a complicated network of codes; codes are acquired and have social and historical aspects. Roland Barthes, the French mythologist, provides a sort of fivefold classification from the codes involved in the semantic mechanism of a text. Barthes's codes include hermeneutic, semantics, symbolic, proairetic and cultural codes. Simurgh which is Shahnameh's mythical-legendary bird raises Zāl, Rostam is born with her tact and through her help, Rostam's wounds are healed in combat with Esfandiyār. She ensures Rostam's victory by warning him that the only weapon that can affect Esfandiyār is a shot to his eyes. This article is intended to decode Simurgh's performance in Shahnameh in accordance with Barthes's fivefold classification.

The next research work is *"A Barthesian Demythologization of a Colonial Painting"* is presented by Peter Gonsalves. The article investigates a painting that was commissioned by the members of the British East India Company and installed in the central hall of their office in London. After establishing its historical context, the text employs Barthesian theory to unravel the cultural, symbolical and hermeneutical myths underpinning the ideology that sustained and promoted the colonial enterprise for more than a century.

The following work is chosen for review is about narrative structure. The Title of research is *"Tracing Eurydice: Adaptation and Narrative Structure in the Orpheus Myth"* is presented by Ryan Cadrette. This thesis hypothesizes an operational technique of critical analysis into the procedures of narrative alteration by scrutinizing the constancies and breaches of a story as it moves across the representative system. for accomplishing this, the researcher draws upon the process of structuralist textual inquiry employed by Barthes in his essay *S/Z* to yield a relative study of three versions of the Orpheus myth from Ovid's *Metamorphoses*.

The study is conducted by rereading the five codes of connotation labeled by Barthes through the lens of the currently adopted theory.

The next work is *"Analysing Tariq Rahman's Story The Dance of the Beards in the Light of Barthes' Narrative Codes"* is presented by Muhammad Saleem. Rahman''s story is being analyzed in the light of poststructural approach to narratology stated by Roland Barthes. The research aims at critical execution of the creation, characters' role. The functions of the five Barthesian codes such as Proairetic, Hermeneutic, Semic, Symbolic and Cultural. The interconnectedness of these narrative codes permits them to overlap one another in order to establish a comprehensible text as they are thought to be in Barthesian vocabulary. It is taken as basic material to the comprehension of any cultural invention as an inventive part.

The last work which is reviewed by the researcher is *"Barthesian Narrative Codes as a Technique for the Analysis of Attar's 'Sheikh San'an"* is designed by the Parvin Telli and Meisam Mahdiar. The researchers examine Sheikh San'an in terms of Roland Barthes's theory of five codes. The main reason for selecting this approach is to claim that diverse factors like social, cultural and artistic should interact for a creative effort in order to be portrayed.

Chapter 03

Theoretical Framework

3.1 Background

Ferdinand de Saussure is considered the originator of structuralism. And the subsequent Moscow, Copenhagen and Prague schools of linguistics endow much to the originator and his book, *Course in General Linguistics,* The core concepts in structural theory are the distinctions between langue and parole and pair of binary oppositions. Structuralism, summarized by Simon Blackburn, "the belief that phenomena of human life that is not intelligible except through their interrelations. The relation constitutes a structure, and behind local variations in the surface phenomena, there are constant laws of abstract culture" (Blackburn, 2008). Structuralism had been defined by Levi Strauss as " a search for the underlying patterns of thought in all forms of human activity" (Doland, 2009).

Structural linguists hold that all the objects of human or social sciences are relational to each other rather than substantial, and they practice, a critical method of inquiry into and analyzing the structures. Claude Levi Strauss, applied Saussurian linguistics to explore the cultural phenomena. He states that we can study the culture in terms of language, a system of signs. Another important structuralist and linguist, Roman Jacobson, who believes that language is governed by an abstract system named binary opposition, which guides meaning in the structure of a narrative. Greimas holds the belief that there are two aspects of an entity, namely its opposite and its negation, which are the elementary structure in our recognition and distinction. Todorov, a French structuralist, states that structures are inherent in any literary discourse. He writes that any narrative is consist of three parts, the verbal (language), the semantics (content) and the syntactic (plot).

The units of language gain meaning from binary oppositions in the system of the narrative. It is not a contradictory relation but a structural, complementary relation (Fagarty, 2005). It is a vital notion of structuralism. Saussure says that meaning of a sign is derived from its context, its syntagmatic dimension and the group or paradigm to which it belongs (Lacey, 200). Saussure believes that any language can be viewed, explored and analyzed as a formal system of differences, dependent on each other for value and meanings. For example, the value of "slave owner" is dependent on the existence of "slave" that was produced by the slavery of the United States; the signifier— "the slave owner" will lose its value without the existence of "slave". Therefore, any one word or sentence in the language system is not self-sufficient in meanings. Tyson states, "Structuralism is a human science which tries to understand, in a systematic way, the fundamental structures that underlie all human experience and, therefore, all human behavior and production" (2006, P. 209-210). Literature is the product of culture, which is one of the human experiences that structuralism seeks to comprehend. The researcher studies, and explores the underlying structure of a literary text. He discovers the hidden codes/rules/ principals that shape a particular text. The meaning of a text is of secondary importance for a structuralist.

In structural analysis, two major styles are derived from Ferdinand de Saussure concepts of syntagmatic and paradigmatic pivots. Propp adopts sequential structural analysis, which is based on the sequence of events, a term derived from syntax. On the other hand, Claude Levi Strauss adopts vertical analysis, which is derived from vertical analysis of the language. It is diachronic rather than synchronic structural analysis. It merely shows the obvious side of the selected text but diachronic analysis digs the hidden side of the story. It extracts the components of the text then discovers the relation among the components and finally indicates an implication within the generality of the text.

Scholes (1985, P.4) states that "…structuralism is a way of looking for reality not individually but in the relationships among them. And facts are states of affairs". Objects fit into one another like the links of a chain and stand in a determinate relationship with one another. The form is the possibility of structure. The structure of a fact consists of the structures of states of affairs.

Wittgenstein,1953). As far as structuralism in literature is concerned, Scholes says, "structuralism tries to establish for literary studies a basis that is as scientific as possible and at the heart of the idea of structuralism is the idea of system: a complete, self-regulating entity that adapts to new conditions by transforming its features while retaining its systematic structure"(1985, P.10). Putting it in a simpler way, Structuralism "attempts to explain the structures underlying literary texts either in terms of a grammar modeled on that of language or in terms of Ferdinand de Saussure's principle that the meaning of each word depends on its place in the total system of language" (Harris 1992, P.378). Jean-Marie Benoist explains the application of structuralism on literature in such way "An analysis is structural if, and only if, it displays the content as a model, i.e. if it can isolate a formal set of elements and relations in terms of which it is possible to argue without entering upon the significance of the given content" (1978, P.8). The formal set of elements are the smallest meaningful units in a work and the mythemes or deep structures of a text (Mc Manus 1998). They say that by virtue of their asceticism certain Buddhists came to see a whole country in a bean. This is what the first analysts of the rest wanted to do: to see all the stories in the world…in one single structure. "We are going, they thought, to extract from each tale its model then from these models we will make a great narrative structure, which we will apply (for verification) to any story in existence – an exhausting task… and finally, an undesirable one, because the text thereby loses its difference". (Barthes 1976, P.7).

3.2. Structuralism and Post-structuralism

Before structuralism, readers and writers believed that a text is a representation of the author's self and it should imply a sense of truth but, Barthes in his seminal essay *The Death of the Author* which was published in 1967 expressed a daring idea that the author and the writing are unrelated and we should not incorporate with intentions and biographical context of an author in an interpretation of a text, because the text is written by an author, is not the sole product of him/her, but a mixture of other texts that are 'always already written' (cf. Barthes 1977). According to this theory after generating a literary text, the author dies and his death gives birth to the reader.

Structuralism is a way of comprehending how language operates as a system of meaning construction. It deals with the various kinds of questions like: How does language function as a kind of meaning machine? The work of Ferdinand de Saussure, *Course in General Linguistics* (1915), makes an ultimate distinction between langue and parole, langue is the social aspect of language that we all draw upon to speak and it is the object of linguistic study, but *parole* is the individual realization of the system in actual instances of language. In his view, words are not symbols but rather are a mark, either written or spoken, called a signifier, and a concept called a signified. The relation between signifier and signified is arbitrary. Language is one among many sign-systems, the science of such systems is called 'semiotics or semiology, and this system is based on differences, that is to say, each sign is distinguished from the other sign because of the differences that exist between them.

Saussure believed that "A linguistic system is a series of differences of sound combined with a series of differences of ideas." He further says, "In language, there are only differences *without positive terms.*" If we take signifiers and signifieds as separate systems, but there is always a tendency on the part of signified to seek its own signifier and to form with it a positive unit, Saussure had recognized that signifier and signified is two separate systems, but he did not see how unstable units of meaning can be when the systems come together (cf. Saussure 1959).

Poststructuralist study the essentially 'unstable' nature of signification. As a cyclic process, each signifier refers to several signifieds and those signifieds themselves will be other signifiers that refer to other signifieds. In this way, we have Derrida's concept of '*différance*' having a concept that the French word different means both to defer and to differ. So in this sense meaning can be never reached. For structuralists, the focus is on *langue* which is the social aspect of language, so they had excluded subjective processes by which individuals interact with each other. In Poststructuralists instead of inspecting language as an impersonal system, one must regard it as always articulated with other systems and especially with subjective processes. They regard language as the coming together of infinite discourses that are so interwoven in each other.

Poststructuralist thought was often taken in the form of a critique of empiricism and metaphysics. These two ideas saw the subject as the source of all knowledge, for them the process of cognition and understanding was from the subject to the human mind. Poststructuralists believed that Knowledge is always formed from discourses which pre-exist the subject's experiences. Paul de Man mentioned Heidegger's views about the epistemological nature of all interpretation in his essay *Form and Intent in American New Criticism,* "No new set of relationships is added to an existing reality, but relationships *that were already there* are being disclosed, not only in themselves (like the events of nature) but as they exist for us" (de Man 1971: 29). Here we can understand that we have reached an "epistemological knowledge that has reversed the order of metaphysics ... An object can never intrude perceptual consciousness of a person, and it cannot be considered as a source for one's consciousness" (Hashemi 2004:

13). The process of understanding is now from the human mind to the outer world.

3.3. S/Z: An Approach to Narrative Analysis

Roland Barthes was born in 1915 and he was a French literary critic. His methods go far beyond semiology. The analytical technique with which the present study is concerned comes from his large 1970 essay *S/Z*, an exhaustive analysis of Sarrasine. Barthes divided the text of *Sarrasine* into 561 pieces, or 'lexias,' which vary in size from one word (as in the case of the title) to several sentences. One lexia is taken for multiple analysis. Barthes analyses each segment for five codes to working underlyingly. He formulates five codes, each has different root an aspect of a literary piece. The first code is the hermeneutic code, which deals with proposing, sustaining and final resolution of the enigmas. There are small enigmas which are exposed and solved quickly and there are major enigmas which are prolonged to the end of the narrative, to keep the interest of the reader. The second code is the semic code which unfolds characters and personalities. It is the voice of the author. The symbolic code revolves around the binary opposition and their relations to the meaning of the text. The proairetic code is the basic code. It is the logic temporal order of events in the text. Which make up the plot of the story.

The researcher studies the narrative of *The Kite Runner* structurally. Theory of five codes is applied and five dimensions are explored. It is found that the selected text is enigmatic for the reader. It is strengthened by the actions of suspense besides having many symbolic and cultural references. The interpretation of the present text by using the lens of Barthian codes can give an insight into the structure of the text. The primary purpose of art is the creation of beauty and the primary purpose of beauty is to give pleasure.

Derrida debates about the meaning of the text and its relation with the structure in his famous work, *Of Grammatology*. He states that there no center of meaning because language is a system of references. Meaning are achieved only through binary opposition within the structure of a text. Barthes in his seminal work *S/Z* (1970) proposed that every text can be analyzed from five codes. They are voices in the text. Every text contains multi-voices inherently. So meanings are not important but the structure of a text is worthwhile to discover the construction of the text. In Death of the Author, he states that "it is a language which speaks, not the author" (Barthes, 1977, P.143). Barthes says the reader is also responsible as much as the author in determining the meanings of a text. In such a way he challenges the traditional literary criticism. The reader gets paramount importance. The text contains plurality and migration of meaning. He argues elsewhere that "every line of written text is a mere reflection of references from a multitude of traditions... the text is nothing but a tissue of quotations drawn from the innumerable centers of culture" (Barthes, 1977, P.146).

3.3 Research Design

The researcher takes the text of the novel the kite runner written by Khaled Hosseini and used a qualitative approach to analyze the work. Bogdan and Taylor (1975, P. 5) define "qualitative methodology as a research procedure that produces descriptive data such as written words or verbal expression from the people and their behavior that have been observed". The researcher takes sampling text for detailed analysis. Barthes Five codes are applied. The researcher divides the analysis into five chapters and a conclusion.

3.3.1. Source of the Data

The researcher collects data from the novel the kite runner written by Khaled Hosseini

3.3.2 Sampling:

There are 25 chapters in the novel of *The Kite Runner*. The researcher takes the whole text for detailed qualitative analysis. The text is surfed from five dimensions to explore the narrative structure.

Data Collection Procedure

1. Researcher reads the entire novel, *The kite runner* keeping in mind the problem and the angle to be analyzed. the researcher intensively read in order to comprehend the text fully.

2. There are 25 chapters of the novel. The researcher takes the whole text for detailed analysis.

3. Researcher breaks down the selected text in various Lexias. And put them in the form of a table.

4. The researcher also reads other reference books related to the topic. Some of them help the researcher identifying the problem of the research.

5. Then the researcher also takes some help and identifies some references from the websites.

3.3.4 Data Analysis Procedure

❖ Researcher divides the analysis into five subchapters and a final conclusion, according to the five codes.

❖ The Classification of the codes are made into sub categories i.e. Hermeneutic Code, Proairetic Code, Semic code, Semantic code, Connotative Code, Cultural Code, and Symbolic Code.

❖ The researcher classifies the codes Answering the problem of the research.

❖ The researcher analyzes the code and its relation to the meanings.

❖ Last but not least after analyzing the codes, the researcher draws the conclusion.

According to Barthes, meanings are dependent on the binary opposition of the signifiers in the text. And multi-meanings can be achieved by the reader. "meaning cannot be determined by an author, but it must actively be shaped by the reader during the process of text analysis. In such an analysis, different codes should be considered for a text that each of its own parts forms the text. In his opinion, the codes will result in an interwoven text" (Sadeghi, Bita: P.65). there is a complex relationship between the producer of the text and the reader of the text.

The search for fixed meaning, given by the author is misleading. the meaning is also created by the reader. "The codes themselves are a set of rules under which elements are selected that are combined with other elements to make new ones" (Miremadi, 2005: P.73).

Barthes opines that an ideal text holds various interpretations and does not limit meaning. The present study takes the narrative of The Kite Runner and applies five codes theory of Roland Barthes to explore the narrative structure. The researcher finds that text can be interpreted from different sides. It contains multi-voices.

3.4 Readerly/ Writerly Text

In *S/Z,* Roland Barthes proposes a difference between what he calls the 'readerly' and 'writerly' text. He suggests that "the goal of literary work (of literature as work) is to make the reader no longer a consumer but a producer of the text and its user, between its owner and customer, between its author and its reader" (Barthes, 1970, P.4). The vast majority of literature that can be purchased at bookstores consists of 'readerly' texts, where the reader is simply consuming the text with little or no reflection. The 'writerly' text, however, allows a multitude of interpretations and it is the reader, along with the writer, who creates and interprets the narrative. This is also related to Barthes' famous idea of 'the death of the author' since, as Barthes himself puts it, "The birth of the Reader must be at the cost of the death of the Author" (P.148). With this quote, Barthes intended to encourage a new era of literature where the reader, once it is written, has more power over work than the author himself. "With structuralism came the idea that works of literature could not be attributed to the genius of a single author. Instead, it was the overall system of writing that had created the work" (Dale Parker, P. 57). No text was truly original since it had to rely on previously established genre conventions and writings. Barthes, being the major figure of the literary theory of structuralism, commercialized this concept in his foundational essay *The Death of the Author*. One example of a 'writerly' text could arguably be the postmodern novel. Postmodernism, which Frederic Jameson referred to as "the cultural logic of late capitalism" (Dale Parker, P.299), has been a philosophical, artistic and cultural intellectual development that succeeded modernism. Postmodern literature brought, according to Glenn Ward in his book *Postmodernism*, "an end to strict divisions between high and low culture, popularized metafiction, and intertextuality, and blurred the boundaries between fact and fiction "(P. 33).

3.5 The Meaning and the Text

According to French philosopher Jacques Derrida (1930-2004), since the time of Plato Western philosophy is based on metaphysical assumptions. 'logocentrism' is closely related to these assumptions. It is a belief that there are an absolute reality and a center of truth or reality that can serve as the basis for all our thoughts and actions. Logocentrism at its core has the notion of 'transcendental signified' which is an external point of reference that will provide the ultimate meaning. Poststructuralists argued that there is no transcendental signified and no ultimate meaning. The meaning is always delayed because each signified is actually a signifier that leads to other signifieds so we have an infinite regress. We can no longer believe that we have one meaning or a Meta meaning, what we have is a set of meanings that are interwoven and inseparable (cf. Derrida 1976).

Barthes puts forward the same idea in S/Z. He introduces the notion of 'writerly text' as a kind of text that allows this infinite number of meanings to coexist and sets some boundaries that allow the reader to look for the meaning and co-create the meaning within those boundaries. He creates five codes (the boundaries) that function as a roadmap for the readers. These five codes are voices that give the writerly text its polyphonic quality. These five voices are the voice of truth, the voice of empirics, the voice of a person, the voice of symbols and the voice of science.

Sarrasine is written by Balzac. Sarrasine is a sculptor, who wins a competition and then goes to Rome, where at a theatre he sees Zambinella and instantly falls in love with her. He thinks that Zambinella is an ideal woman. He plans and then abducts her from a party. Sarasate refuses to believe on cardinal who told him that Zembinella is a castrato. When Zambinella confirms about his identity, Sarrasine is about to kill him but cardinal's men stab Sarrasine.

Barthes states that modern and avant-garde text are writerly text which is open to interpretations. They allow the reader to participates in the production of the text.

3.6. Barthes' Theory of Five Codes

"Barthes presents his theory of five codes to understand the underlying structure of a text. He proposed that these five codes are the basic underlying structures of all narratives" (Barry, 2002, p.151). A literary text which is an artistic piece has five codes underlyingly. Roland Barthes exposes the blocks of text under the heading Lexia. These are like semantic wrappings, " the best possible space in which we can observe meanings" (S/Z, P. 13). The text is divided into five codes, and these lexia have a " specific effect, or function different from that of neighboring stretches of text" (Culler, 1975, P. 202). Codes enable the researcher to dissect the text into different layers. Barthes states that lexia division is not prescribed for all analysis. Barthes points out the inherent pluralistic and subjective nature of meaning in literary work. In S/Z, Barthes provides evidence that even a classic text such as *Sarrasine* has the multiplicity and instability of meanings. Each code is associated with a voice. Barthes argues how "semiologically, each connotation is the starting point of the code, the articulation of a voice which is woven into the text" (S/Z, P. 9). First two codes are closely related to enigma and the actions. They form a narrative structure in the text. They are readerly or passive. They are sequential, temporal and logical. They are syntagmatic and other three are paradigmatic in nature.

3.6.1 Proairetic Code

It is a code of actions which denotes events and situation in logical sequence and order in the text. It proposes an action, then develops the action to the climax and then finally finds the resolution of the narrative. It is natural that readers anticipate completion of the action that was started in the text. When the execution of the reader is not meted out, tension is created in the mind of the reader. He reads further to remove the tension. It is called suspense in the text, expectation of what to happen and desire of completion of a started action. It hooks the attention of the reader. Every action trigger subsequent actions. The reader waits for the next action and completion of the action. It is a syntagmatic study. the rest of the codes are free from this restraint of logic temporal order. They are understood paradigmatically. "Therefore, these codes are studied syntagmatically. The rest of the codes   are   free   from the chronological order and thus can be understood paradigmatically" (Ali, 2013, p.120). This code is closely related to the text's narrative structure. Barthes notes, "the discourse, rather than the characters determine the action" (S/Z p. 18). An action is composed of data, which represents the sequence. "By naming these actions, an author expresses their signification through recognition of the already written, seen, read (for example, to stroll, to murder, to rendezvous)" (S/Z p.19). Barthes references an example of an action in Balzac's text in lexia 6, " and hidden behind the sinuous folds of a silk curtain" (*S/Z*, P. 21). It is the way such details are organized or ordered that facilitate the plot or actions, in order to impart meaning. Barthes comments that "in Aristotelian terms, praxis is linked to proairetic, or the ability rationally to determine the result of an action" (*S/Z*, P. 18).

3.6.2 Hermeneutic Code

It is also called the code of engimas and The code of puzzles. It questions, it aporias and creates suspense and enigma. This code not only structures the narrative but it also "generates various strategies and devices aimed at capturing and maintaining the reader's interests" (Ribière, 2008, p.46). we can explore this code at the early pages of the text. It deals with mysterious, unexplained or incomplete puzzling elements in the narrative. It creates curiosity to know the secret or to find the answer of the enigma. gradually the reply or answer is unveiled and sometimes delays the answers. Sometimes misleading answers are given to deceive the reader. In Barthes terms, these elements are termed as "snare", "equivocation", "jamming" and "suspended answers". The term snare refers to "deliberate evasion of the truth', and the term equivocation stands for 'mixture of truth and snare" (S/Z 1970.p.). Some of the enigmatic elements are exposed at the end of the text while some of them remain a covert for the reader. "The reader uses his/her mental faculty to give meaning to the text" (Felluga, n.d.).

Barthes defines this category as containing the story's main structure and "units whose function it is to articulate, in various ways, a question, its response, and the variety of chance events which can either formulate the question or delay its answer" (S/Z, P. 17). Elements of the text that contribute to the hermeneutic level include devices which "project, define, reveal or solve a mystery" (*S/Z*, P. 17). For example, in S/Z, Barthes, raises questions about the real identity and meanings of the title, who or what is Sarrasine? This is not done through the the actual word, but by its connotation (a drift away from the word) – the isolation of the word without a context immediately produces a puzzle and so may prompt curiosity in the reader. The mystery was introduced in the very title of the story. We learn much later in Balzac's story that this very femininity is questionable, so a reference to a further mystery is subtly introduced in the title. A second enigma is highlighted by Barthes in lexia 14, referencing a section from Balzac's text, "people must have a huge fortune", stating that the wealth of the family referred to is indicated here, but the source of this wealth is later questioned (*S/Z*, P.30-31).

3.6. 3. Cultural Code

It is also called the code of reference. It is the references of sciences and arts of the real world. All lexicalized knowledge, linguistic knowledge, beliefs or culture, and society. It works as a background to construct the structure of the text. It is the voice of science in the narrative. These are references to "types of knowledge that offer scientific or moral authority or a body of knowledge, for example, 'physical, physiological, medical, psychological, literary, historical" (*S/Z, P.* 20). It is the knowledge possessed by all members of society. It is shared data among all persons of culture. It represents conventional, traditional or cultural knowledge prevalent in society. Barthes in his book S/Z at lexia 11 to states an example of the referential "...a splendid salon decorated in silver and gold, with glittering chandeliers, sparkling with candles. There, milling about, whirling around, flitting here and there, were the most beautiful women of Paris, the richest, the noblest, dazzling, stately, resplendent with diamonds, flowers in their hair, on their bosoms, on their heads, strewn over dresses or in garlands at their feet." He further mentions, " Light, rustling movements, voluptuous steps, made the laces, the silk brocades, the gauzes, float around their delicate forms". He points out the social and ethnic references. "One might also catch movements of the head meaningful to lovers and negative gestures for husbands". The story describes the voices of gamblers at the dice, the sound of the gold, which is mingling with music and murmur of conversation of people.

"…and to complete the giddiness of this mass of people intoxicated by everything seductive the world can hold, a haze of perfume and general inebriation played upon the fevered mind". Barthes identifies referential links in this lexia; which he describes as 'ethnicity' and 'psychology', stating "an adulterous ambiance is designated'; and 'it connotes Paris as an immoral city" (*S/Z*, P. 25).

3.6. 4. The Semantic Code

It is also called the connotative string of the text. It is abbreviated as SEM by the Barthes. It is called the voice of the author in the text. It is often found around characterization. "This code is also related to the theme "(Barry, 2002, p.151).

Nichols (1985) holds that "the semic codes let us label persons and places in a narrative in an adjectival way" (p.480). Connotations of a text are the fruit and the essence of it. Semic code – "the voice of the person"'Semantically, the seme is the unit of the signifier" (*S/Z*, P. 17). This connotation is, according to Barthes, implied "nearby' 'a correlation immanent in the text'*'(S/Z*, P. 8). This code is basically metonymic, what is implied rather than explicitly stated. For example, the statement "in the trenches', may stand in for/be associated with, amongst other things, to be in battle during the First World War. Semes can be expressed and indicated without any order or link with a character, place or object – they are 'flickers" (*S/Z*, P. 19). However, understanding and comprehension mostly rely on the cultural values behind the text. Barthes accepts that all interpretation is culturally referenced. It also destabilizes the fixed meaning of the text because meaning is depended on binary opposition within the text and their cultural significance outside the text.

3.6. 5. Symbolic Code

It is abbreviated as SYM by the Barthes in his analysis of *Sarrasine.* It deals with binaries in the text. Binary opposition is pivotal to the creation of any text. It is also called the antithetic code. It deals with thesis and antithesis. "The concept of polarities or binary oppositions is central to the theory of Structuralism. By these binary oppositions, a structuralist understands reality" (Barry, 2002, p.151). it is the voice of the symbol, the code refers to the symbolic patterns in the narrative, as in Sarrasine it is done through antithesis and opposition or mediation and conjunction. Barthes example," lexia two states the symbol is represented by the mediation of inside/outside, shown in Balzac's text as 'then turning in the other direction' (between the garden and the house)" (*S/Z*, P. 24). Another example of symbolic patterns found across Balzac's text is through what Barthes describes as the " 'axis of castration' – relating to gender ambiguity – which is a recurring theme in Balzac's story. These symbolic groupings create links which are dispersed throughout the text, creating a non-linear network of meaning, which can accordingly 'be entered from any number of points and are reversible and multivalent"(*S/Z*, P. 19).

3.7. Five Codes As Five Voices

According to Barthes, "these five codes create a kind of network, topos through the entire text passes'. The convergence of the voices (of the codes) becomes writing, a stereographic space where the five codes, the five voices intersect" (P. 21). Each code has a different perspective of the narrative.

3.7.1. The voice of truth (the Hermeneutic code)

any question, puzzle, enigma or discrepancy distinguished, suggested, formulated and held in suspense in the narrative which should   be   disclosed   in   the   end.

3.7.2. The Voice of Empirics (the Proairetic code)

It is the code of action. It builds interest and suspense throughout the narrative. It starts actions, then further triggers actions and finally completes the actions. It is the voice of empirics. It follows a logico-temporal sequence. It is a syntax of the narrative. It works in collaboration with the hermeneutic code.

3.7.3. The voice of Symbols (the Symbolic code)

It is closely related to a binary opposition. It gives meaning by opposite signifiers.

3.7.4. The voice of a person (the Semic code)

It is related with connotative meanings of the text. It is the voice of the author. It is related to the supernatural, romantic and abnormal situation and incidents. It is related to the characters and their inherent motifs

3.7.5. The voice of Science (the Cultural Codes)

It is the voice of the common knowledge prevalent in culture and society. It is a general understanding of the community. All references to the history, philosophy, psychology, religion, and literature belong to this code.

3.8. Conclusion

Barthes follows a method of analysis in his book S/Z. first, he cut the whole text in small units of 561 called, lexia. Second, lexia is taken as the unit of analysis. The size of lexia is not fixed as it could be a word or phrase or a whole paragraph. Then he applied all codes on lexias. It is also possible that one lexia holds more than one code. All the narrative codes are abbreviated into ACT, HER, SEM, SYM, and REF.

The present thesis studies the text of The Kite Runner written by Khaled Hosseini qualitatively. It is based on the seminal book of Roland Barthes, *S/Z.* in the book Barthes analyses the novella of Balzac, Sarrasine. He divides the text of Sarrasine into lexias, for detailed analysis. The researcher does not divide the whole text into lexias, instead, whole text studies to find out the relevant lexia to prove the point to view adopted. The researcher divides the analysis into sub five parts according to the five codes then each code is explored through the text of the novel.

Chapter 04

Barthesian Reading of

The Kite Runner

(Data Analysis)

It is the most important chapter of the thesis as it shows the application of the five codes on the selected text, *The Kite Runner* written by an Afghan writer, Khaled Hosseini. The present chapter is further divided into five subchapters according to the five codes. each chapter explores one code. Barthes states in his seminal work *S/Z* that all narratives are interwoven with multiple voices. Any text is in fact marked by multiple meanings suggested by five codes. Together, these five codes function as a "weaving of voices," as Barthes puts it (P.20). The codes point to the "multivalence of the text" and to "its partial reversibility" (P.20), "allowing a reader to see a work not just as a single narrative line but as a constellation or braiding of meanings: "The grouping of codes, as they enter into the work, into the movement of the reading, constitute a braid (text, fabric, braid: the same thing); each thread, each code, is a voice; these braided or braiding, voices from the writing" (S/Z, 1970, P.160). This study examines the five codes which Barthes has introduced in his *S/Z* (1970) work, as the manifestation of the structuralist notion, elaborating the idea that, each of these codes functions as a distinct but interrelated voice in studying *The Kite Runner*. The study at hand focuses on each of these codes separately to show their pattern and then discusses the ways through which these codes create a polyphonic whole that allows the reader to be a participant in the process of moving toward the possible meanings.

4.1. The Exploration of Proairetic Code (ACT)

The researcher explores the text, *The Kite Runner* by Khalid Hosseini under the light of the Proairetic code given by Roland

Barthes. This part of the thesis studies the series of actions and tension in the plot which help the t to move towards its destination. Barthes claims that every text possesses five codes underlying (Hermeneutic code, Proairetic code, Symbolic code, Cultural code, and Semantic code). The researcher starts the analysis of the text under the shadow of Proairetic code. This code is also called a code of action and code of narrative. "In the narrative, however, the discourse, rather than the characters, determines the action" (Barthes, p. 18).

The Proairetic code implies action which suggests further actions. It creates tension in the text and gives its resolution. It makes the reader attentive and creates suspense related to the action. The study finds out that the story starts with the action of the phone call from Rahim Khan. The action of Rahim Khan compels Amir to go back to Afghanistan, where his redemption waits for him. So text starts with an action, then that action is followed by a sequence of actions leading to its final resolution. One action gives birth to another action. The novel deals with the junction of actions woven together to give it a shape.

4.1.1. Data Analysis

The Kite Runner is set primarily in Afghanistan, but it also includes chapters set in America and Pakistan. Spanning a time period from roughly 1973–2002, *The Kite Runner* begins with an anonymous narrator reflecting on the ways his past have shaped his personality and life. He struggles with guilt over decisions he made as a child, and many things in his adult life trigger this guilt. He tells his story, beginning with the recollection of his childhood servant and playmate Hassan, whose loyal friendship he never quite deserved.

Twelve-year-old Amir lives in a wealthy district of Kabul and is raised by his father, Baba, with help from Ali, the servant and his son Hassan. Amir and Hassan often play together like brothers, yet both are aware that they occupy different classes in society. Their relationship is also complicated by Amir's jealousy of the fatherly attention Hassan receives from both Ali and Baba.

The Proairetic code is the voice of empirics refers to those elements that generate anticipation and tension in the text and clasps the curiosity of the reader. It deals with the series of actions which forms the plot of the novel. In the novel from the very start till end, Proaeritic code helps to propel the story.

In chapter one, Rahim Khan requests Amir and asks him to come back from California to Pakistan & Afganistan. The phone call is the first and vital action which pushes the story towards its next action. "One-day last summer, my friend Rahim Khan called from Pakistan. He asked me to come to see him. Standing in the kitchen with the receiver to my ear, I knew it wasn't just Rahim Khan on the line. It was my past of unatoned sins" (Hosseini, p. 1). The phone call from Rahim Khan is taken as summon from the past of Amir. Amir's sins from his past call him towards them. The action of this phone call from Rahim Khan creates interest in the mind of readers. It creates strain in the plot of the text. This action triggers the story to move forward.

In chapter number two, there is a flashback of the childhood of Hassan and Amir. The actions of Hassan and Amir reflect the deep friendship among them. It develops the plot of the text further by presenting the friendship of Hassan and Amir through their joyful engagements. "When we were children, Hassan and I used to climb the poplar trees in the driveway of my father's house and annoy our neighbors by reflecting sunlight into their homes with a shard of the mirror" (Hosseini, p. 3). In these lines, Proairetic code helps the plot to move forward. As these lines show Amir and Hassan use to spent their childhood with each other. Hassan and Amir climb the poplar tree and use to annoy neighbor by reflecting the light of the sun with the help of a mirror. They enjoy their naughty moments by teasing others. Their actions of teasing others and the solace which they find with each other let the readers know about their friendship.

By this narrative code focuses on actions and stipulates its reactions. This creates curiosity in the readers and forces them to think about further action. In chapter three Amir communicates with his father about the teachings of Mullah Fatiullah Khan. His father's actions and gestures develop actions in the story. Readers have anticipated the reaction of Amir's father.

We were upstairs in Baba's study, the smoking room when I told him what Mullah Fatiullah had taught us in class. Baba was pouring himself a whiskey from the bar he had built in the corner of the room. He listened, nodded, took a sip from his drink. Then he lowered himself into the leather sofa, put down his drink, and propped me up on his lap. I felt as if I were sitting on a pair of tree trunks. He took a deep breath and exhaled through his nose, the air hissing through his mustache for what seemed an eternity. I couldn't decide whether I wanted to hug him or leap from his lap in mortal fear (Hosseini, p. 16).

In these lines, Amir talks about his guilt with his father. On hearing this Amir's father remains silent. He remains busy with his whiskey. He takes the drink, his actions are serious and his breath seems endless. Amir feels fear from his father that he is unable to decide whether he should hug his father with the fear of him or he should jump off. This scene creates tension. Agha's actions seem serious and subtle. But further the tension is resolved and readers come to know that he gives an answer to Amir in a polite manner.

The roles of the narrative code are to make the reader attentive and interested in the plot. In the start of chapter five, there is gunshots and the sound of fire outside the house. "Something roared like thunder the rat-a-tat-tat of gunfire. "Father!" Hassan cried". We sprung to our feet and raced out of the living room. We found Alihobbling frantically across the foyer "(Hosseini, p. 33). The gunfire and shoots make the reader inquisitive. Their action of running towards the living room to secure them indicates the insecurity in Afghanistan. It creates motion in the plot. These gunshots and fires create surprising elements for the readers. These gunshots predicted terror and panic condition which is soon appearing on the surface of Afghanistan. The terror, on the one hand, reveals the scenario of Afghanistan and on the other hand further the action in the novel and consequently, it forces Amir and his father to leave Afghanistan. Researcher explores The narrative code of actions which is interwoven in the text. In chapter number six, the key event is introduced which is the kite running tournament.

Amir hopes to finally impress Baba by winning a kite-fighting tournament. In Afghanistan, kite fighting is a serious sport. In the tournament kites made of bamboo and colorful thin paper are flown by teams made up of two males. Cutting down someone's kite depends on the skill of the flier and such factors as the flexibility of the kite's bamboo frame and how hard the wind blows. Any kite that is cut free can be confiscated. When an opponent's kite is cut down, one member of the team becomes the kite runner who finds and claims the kite. When Amir cuts down the kite of his final opponent, Hassan runs to retrieve it. Amir goes looking for him, and he finds him trapped in an alleyway by three bullies.

The actions of flying kite and chasing them play a crucial role in the life of both friends. "I remember one overcast winter day, Hassan and I were running a kite. I was chasing him through neighborhoods, hopping gutters, weaving through narrow streets. I was a year older than him, but Hassan ran fast than I did, and I was falling behind" (Hosseini, p, 49). These lines indicate the actions of Hassan and Amir which exposes their bond. The plot moves forward through their action of chasing kites. Although Amir is one year elder than Hassan Hassan is quick and fast than him. Amir falls behind him. The code of action portrays that morally

Aamir has fallen behind. These action help readers come to know about another event of the plot.

"Assef knelt behind Hassan, put his hands on Hassan's back and undid his own belt buckle with his free hand. He unzipped his jeans. Dropped his underwear. He positioned himself behind Hassan. Hassan did not struggle. Didn't even whimper. He moved his head slightly and I caught a glimpse of his face. Saw the resignation in it. It was a look I had seen before. It was the look of the lamb" (Hosseini, p. 71).

Two bullies pin his arms while the leader, Assef, rapes him. Paralyzed by fear Amir simply watches. Wanting the kite as a trophy, Amir chooses not to stand up to Assef. He runs away and does not return until Hassan is alone. When Hassan limps up to him with the kite, Amir does not acknowledge what he has seen. These lines indicate the main tension in the plot. This action shows the major tension in the novel. this fold of action boots the plot of the novel and helps further actions to take place.

The Proairetic code which is working underneath is explored. It reveals that rape of Hassan and the inability of Aamir creates guilt in Amir which leads towards crucial actions in the later part of the novel. It is an action which suggests next action and triggers the plot to move on. "… curiously, we call the knot (of the story) what needs to be unknotted (denouement), we situate the knot at the peak of the crisis, not at its outcome" (Barthes, p. 52).

As in the novel, the guilt takes place in the heart of Amir on seeing the rape but not helping him. He calls himself the monster of a dream. The monstrous action gives birth to another monstrous action. "I thought about Hassan's dream, the one about us swimming in the lake. There is no monster, he'd said, just water Except he'd been wrong about that. There was a monster in the lake. It had grabbed by the ankles, dragged him to the murky bottom. I was that monster" (Hosseini, p. 81). Amir associates himself as a monster of Hassan's dream. He links the dragging action of a monster with him and calls him a monster in the life of Hassan as Amir did not help him.

Hassan changes after that, rarely smiling or singing, yet he continues to serve Amir and ask him to hang out. This behavior makes Amir feel so guilty that he can no longer bear to see Hassan every day. He frames Hassan for theft, thinking that would cause Baba to send him away. Although Hassan pretends that he is guilty in order to protect Amir, Baba forgives him. When Ali finds out the truth he decides to leave with Hassan in order to protect him against Amir.

Actions are woven together like threads of the dress. One thread completes another thread and so on. In the novel code of action generates the sequence of actions. Amir plots a trick against Hassan to get him out from his sight as his sight reminds him of the sin of being coward.

"Then I took a couple of the envelopes of cash from the pile of gifts and my watch and tiptoed out. I paused before baba's study and listened in. he'd been in there all morning, making phone calls. He was talking to someone now, about a shipment of rugs due to arrive next week. I went downstairs, crossed the yard, and entered Ali and Hassan's mattress and planted my new watch and a handful of Afghani bills under it. I waited another thirty minutes. Then I knocked on Baba's door and told what I hoped would be the last in a long line of shameful lies" (Hosseini p, 97).

Amir plans to blame Hassan in the theft which his father considers the sin in the world. He takes money, watch and bills to place under the mattress of Hassan. He wants Hassan to be entitled as a thief. He wants his Baba to throw Hassan out as he feels guilt by seeing him. After placing the possession under the mattress. Amir knocks the door of his father's room and tells him about the treacherous action of theft. In this way, Aamir builds one action after another to get rid of his inner uneasiness.

The action of accusing Hassan cause another action. "A few moments later, Baba knocked on my door. "Come to my office," he said. We're all going to sit down and settle this thing" (Hosseini p, 97). Amir's Baba knocks on the door of his room and asks him to come to the office to settle the situation. The incidents make the situation unbearable. Ali decides to leave home. "Life here impossible for us now, Agha sahib. We're leaving." Ali drew Hassan to him, curled his arm around his son's shoulder" (Hosseini p, 98). Ali takes the decision to leave. All wraps him the arm around his son to protect him. This action shows that Ali wants to protect his son from everyone and to leave the house immediately.

The narrative moves forward when Ali and Hassan leave the house. "I watched Alihaul the lone suitcase carrying all of their belongings to Baba's car idling outside the gates. Hassan lugged his mattress, rolled tightly and tied with a rope, on his back"(Hosseini p, 100). In these lines, it is clear that Hassan and Ali leave the house as well as leave the stamp of sin on Amir. Amir watches Ali and Hassan while packing their stuff to leave. Hassan carries the mattress and Hassan drags the suitcase. These actions are the consequences of preceding actions and generate proceeding actions.

A few years later the government of Afghanistan changes when the monarchy is overthrown and a republic is formed. When a communist political party takes over and Soviet troops invade to support the communist party, Afghanistan becomes a very dangerous place, and Amir and his father flee to safety. They move to Pakistan and then to Fremont, California, where they struggle to make a living. While working at a flea market and attending junior college, Amir meets and falls in love with a girl named Soraya. Though suffering from cancer, Baba helps Amir get her father's blessing. A month after Amir and Soraya are married Baba dies.

Code of the action binds the readers with the story. Readers come to know that Amir and his Baba use to live in California peacefully. "I remember the two of us walking through Lake Elizabeth Park in Fremont, a few streets down from our apartment, and watching boys at batting practice, little girls giggling on the swings in the playground" (Hosseini p, 116). These lines indicate the life of California. Amir and his father used to walk through the lake. They watch batting practice of bike and giggling of girls. The life of California and the activities in the city are joyous. These joyous and peaceful activities make them live here.

One day Amir receives a call from his father's old friend Rahim, whom he was always fond of because he encouraged Amir's writing career. Rahim is in Pakistan, and he is dying. He asks Amir to visit him. During their reunion, Rahim tells Amir what has happened since he left, which includes the news that Hassan had married, fathered a boy named Sohrab, and was killed by a militant group called the Taliban that had taken over Afghanistan. Hassan was killed for defending his childhood home. Rahim also reveals that Baba was Hassan's father, which puts more pressure on Amir to rescue his orphaned nephew. "A week later, I sat on a window seat abroad a Pakistan international airlines flight, watching a pair of uniformed airline workers remove the wheel chocks" (Hosseini, p 178). On the response of the call of Rahim Khan, Amir now goes to Pakistan in order to meet him. The action of Rahim compels Amir to go in a flashback to expose his sin to the readers. Now he goes to Pakistan.

The code of narrative creates pull in the text. When Amir meets Rahim Khan, it creates a pull in the story. "I want to tell you about him. I want to tell you everything. You will listen? I nodded. Then Rahim Khan sipped some more tea. Rested his head against the wall and spoke" (Hosseini, p 187). In these lines, Rahim Khan wants to tell Amir about everything, especially about Hassan. He asks Amir to listen to him and Amir shakes his head. Rahim Khan takes tea and rests his head against the wall in order to tell Amir everything.

The narrative code makes the reader the will to redeem himself works as a driving force to run the actions through the novel. "Rahim Khan raised the teacup to his parched lips and took a sip. He then fished an envelope from the breast pocket of his vest and handed it to me (Hosseini p, 199)". These lines show that Rahim Khan thrusts a letter to Amir. This action of handing a letter to Amir makes the readers attentive to know about the further actions in the text. This action helps the narrative to move further and resolve the tension. The letter of Rahim Khan creates tension in the plot that compels Amir to go and help Sohrab, Son of Hassan. "Very well then," Assef said, disdainful. "He shoved Sohrab in the back, pushed him right into the table. Sohrab's hips struck the table, knowing it upside down and spilling the grapes. He fell on them, face first, and stained his shirt purring of brass balls, were now pointing to the ceiling" (Hosseini p, 262). These lines show that Assefbehaves in a very cruel way with Sohrab. He pushes Sohrab in the back that he falls on the bushes. The brutality and cruelty of Assefcompel Amir to take a stand and flee with Sohrab. The tension near to its resolves. Amir returns to Kabul and learns that Sohrab was taken from the orphanage by a Taliban official. The official turns out to be Assef, the childhood bully who had raped Hassan and is now doing the same to his son. To earn Sohrab's freedom Amir agrees to fight Assef. Amir is beaten badly, but the physical pain spiritually heals him.

The code of action implies one action which implies another action. Amir and Sohrab escape from the cage of Assef. "Let's go! Sohrab said. He took my hand. Helped me to my feet. Every inch of my battered body wailed with pain" (Hosseini p, 267). In the resolution of the text, Amir and Sohrabflee from the grip of Assef. Sohrab takes the hand and helps him to run away. Unable to get pregnant yet believing in the importance of family, Soraya is eager to adopt Sohrab. But Amir encounters many difficulties, including Sohrab's attempted suicide, while trying to arrange the boy's immigration to America. Once in America Sohrab does not say a word for nearly a year. Then one day the three are in the park for an Afghan celebration. Amir buys a kite and tries to get Sohrab interested. Together they cut down another kite. Echoing words once uttered by Hassan, Amir vows to be Sohrab's kite runner. In so doing Amir both resurrects the past and sets a path for a new future.

" To depart/to travel/ to arrive/ to stay: the journey is saturated. To end, to fill, to join, to unify. One might say that this is the basic requirement of the readerly, as though it were prey to some obsessive fear: that omitting a connection". The narrative of *The Kite Runner* runs smoothly without any disruption or blanks. It gives a sense of completeness. It begins, it rises, touches the climax and finally finds the resolution of the action. " Fear of forgetting engenders the appearance of a logic of actions; terms and links between them are posited(invented) in such a way that they unite, duplicate each other, create an illusion of continuity"(Barthes, p. 105).

4.1.3. Cod of Action in Summary

Introduction

1. In 2001 Amir gets a phone call from Rahim.

Rising Action

2. Amir recalls a day in his past that changed everything.

3. Amir witnesses the first coup of the Afghanistan government.

4. With Hassan's help, Amir wins a kite-flying tournament.

Climax

5. Too scared to help, Amir witnesses Hassan's assault.

Falling Action

6. Baba and Amir flee Afghanistan for California.

Resolution

7. Amir goes to Afghanistan to find Hassan's orphaned son.

4.1.4. Conclusion

"There is a belief that great structures, serious symbols, grand meanings are built upon an unimpressive foundation of ordinary acts that discourse notes as a matter of form" (Barthes, p. 51). The chapter deals with the exploration of Proairetic code in the text, *The Kite Runner*. The researcher studies the tension and actions in the novel. The researcher applies the theory of narrative given by

Roland Barthes. Roland Barthes gives the five codes theory. According to Roland Barthes, each text has five codes, interwoven together. The theory pacts with the Proairetic code, Hermeneutic code, Symbolic code, Semantic code, and Cultural code. The chapter finds out that the novel deals with tension which creates an interest in the story and also propelled the story of the novel. In the novel characters and actions reveal their relations and nature. " The classic narrative is basically subject to the logical temporal order. writing the end (a phrase which is precisely both temporal and logical) thus posits everything that has been written as having been a tension which naturally requires resolution, a consequence, an end, i.e, something like a crisis" (Barthes, p. 52)

4.2 The Exploration of Hermeneutic Code (HER)

The present chapter studies the novel *The Kite Runner* by Khalid Hosseini through the lens of Barthes' Hermeneutic code. The researcher in the present chapter analyzes the mysterious and puzzling elements in the novel which help in the formation of the text. The study deals with the code of enigma in Hosseini's *The Kite Runner*. The chapter studies the novel *The Kite Runner* through the Hermeneutic code of Barthes. Barthes gives the five codes theory in his book *S/Z*. The codes are, "Hermeneutic code", "Proairetic code", "Symbolic code", "Cultural code" and "Semantic code". The Hermeneutic code is also termed as "Jamming", "Snare" and "Delay" or "Enigma code", The present chapter finds out that hermeneutic code is a crucial code which formulates the plot of the novel. The suspense in the text is maintained through the sin, relationships, friendship, and betrayal which frames the plot and that are unveiled at the end of the novel. As Barthes writes, " Under the hermeneutic code, we list the various (formal) terms by which an enigma can be distinguished, suggested, formulated, held in suspense, and finally disclosed" (P.19)

4.2.1. Data Analysis

The researcher explores the function of the hermeneutic code in the structure of the novel *The Kite Runner*. This code deals with the suspense, queries and mysterious elements which arouses enigma in the mind of the audience. This code helps in the formation of suspense and continuity in the story. The code pacts with such mysterious elements which arise a question in the mind of the reader. " Let us designate as hermeneutic code (HER) all the units whose function it is to articulate in various ways a question, its response, and the variety of chance events which can either formulate the question or delay its answer; or even, constitute an enigma and lead to its solution" (Barthes, p. 17).

The title of the novel, *The Kite Runner* raises questions e.g what it means by the kite runner? who the kiter is?. The Hermeneutic code is involved in the title and also from the start of the book. The book opens in 2001, with the narrator remembering something that happened in 1975, an unnamed event in an alley that "made him who he is today" (Hosseini, p. 01). The memory of this event has continued to haunt Amir for years despite his attempts to escape it. Amir explains that he received a call the summer before from an old friend in Pakistan named Rahim Khan. Amir thinks of Rahim Khan's voice as symbolic of Amir's own past "unatoned sins." Rahim Khan asks Amir to come to see him in Pakistan and tells

Amir "there is a way to be good again"(Hosseini, P.02). Rahim Khan calls Amir and asks him to come to Pakistan. He does not only invite Amir but also gives him some pieces of advice. This line creates the suspense in the story. The readers are forced to think about the advice which Rahim gives to Amir. The question arises in the mind of readers that why does Rahim Khan advices Amir to be good again? Did he do anything wrong? These questions develop in the reader's mind. The readers are compelled to think, why should Amir be good again? These questions compel to know the reason behind this advice.

The hermeneutic code generates curiosity and creates a desire to resolve it. The mystery is developed when Amir narrates about Hassan and his mother. The relationship between Hassan and his mother is mysterious. Amir says, "Hassan never talked about his mother as if she'd never existed" (Hosseini, P. 6). This line elucidates that Hassan does not talk about his mother. He never discusses his feelings about his mother to anyone. He lives without his mother as she does not exist. This strangeness in Hassan develops furtiveness in the story which is needed to be resolved.

The mystery behind the nil feelings of Hassan for his mother pushes the readers to read the story with more interest.

The hermeneutic code is also called the enigmatic code. The enigma of hatred against Ali is created. Questions are raised to find the cause of the insult and hatred for Ali. "Ali's face and his walk frightened some of the younger children in the neighborhood. But the real trouble was with the older kids. They chased him on the street and mocked him when he hobbled by. Some had taken to calling him Babalu, or Boogeyman" (Hosseini, P. 8). In these lines, Ali is treated very badly by the kids. The insult develops puzzle in the text that why does Ali face inappropriate comments? Ali is scorned by children. These insulting comments compel readers to dig out the reason. The curiosity to know about the truth fabricates the interest of readers in the novel. Some of the children mock Ali's appearance and limp and call him *Babalu,* or Boogeyman. After some delay, the enigma of hatred against Ali and Hassan is exposed. Ali and Hassan are Hazaras, an ethnic minority in Afghanistan that is looked down on by the Pashtun majority. The Hazaras have more Asian features, while the

Pashtuns appear more Arabic. Another division between them is that the Hazaras are Shi'a Muslims, while the Pashtuns are Sunni. Amir once read a history book about a Hazara uprising in the nineteenth century, and how the Pashtuns put down the rebellion with "unspeakable violence" (Hosseini p.09). The enigmatic code also creates interest to unveil the truth. In the novel, the reason behind the insulting comments is resolved when the narrator narrates about their Hazara background. Hazaras are ugly and flat nosed. "They called him "flat-nosed" because of Ali and Hassan's characteristic Hazara Mongoloid features" (Hosseini, p. 8). The ugly features of Ali are associated with Hazara sect. Hazaras are insulted because of the sect, they belong. The narrator holds the answer of the puzzle which is created in the reader through the help of Hermeneutic code. The answer to hatred for Hazara people is delayed by the narrator to make more interest in the novel. The hermeneutic code refers to the riddles in the novel. In the fifth chapter of the novel, the mystery is urbanized through the viciousness of Assef with Hassan and Amir. This incident creates mystery in the novel.

Hassan retreated behind me as the three older boys closed in. they stood before us, three tall boys dressed in jeans and T-shirts. Towering over us all, Assef crossed his thick arms on his chest, a savage sort of grin on his lips. Not for the first time, it occurred to me how lucky I was to have baba as my father, the sole reason, I believe, Assefhad mostly refrained from harassing me too much (Hosseini, p. 36-37).

These lines elaborate that Assef and his group of boys threat Hassan. Hassan recoils behind Amir. Hassan is much frightened from Assef. Assefhas a smirk smile when he sees Hassan. But he does not do anything just because of the presence of Amir. Assef feels hatred for Hassan. Assefcontrols himself in the presence of Amir because their fathers are friends. This hatred of Asseffor Hassan forms the question to be resolved.

Amir feels that Baba hates him for killing his mother in childbirth. Baba does not like Amir's pursuits of reading and writing literature. Amir is a terrible player in Baba's favorite sport. Once Amir goes with Baba to watch Buzkashi game, but he badly cries when a rider gets trampled. Amir faces Baba scorn for the incident.

Rahim Khan seems to understand Amir better than his father. Once Baba says to Rahim Khan that Amir is unable to stand for himself. On the other hand, Hassan is liked by Baba. He also likes stories of Amir. Amir often reads to him. In the trunk of the tree, Amir had carved the words "Amir and Hassan, the sultans of Kabul"(Hosseini, P. 27). The boy's favorite story "Rostam and Sohrab," (Hosseini, P. 28) is about the warrior Rostam who kills his enemy in a battle and finally discovers that it is his long lost son Sohrab. It is a tragic story, but Amir feels that all fathers have a secret desire to kill their sons (Hosseini, P. 28). One day Amir pretends to read a story while making up his own story. Hassan says that it is one of the best stories Amir has ever read. Encouraged by the compliments, Amir writes his first ever story of a man who tears turn into pearls. He makes himself painful so he can keep crying and become richer. The story ends with a mountain of pearls, weeping over the wife he has killed. Amir tries to impress the Baba but Baba does not take any interest. However, Rahim Khan encouraged Amir Later that night Rahim Khan leaves Amir a note that says he has a "special talent," (Hosseini, P. 32). Amir is encouraged to keep writing.

Hermeneutic code denotes to the term "Snare". Snare deals with the "deliberate evasion of truth". In the novel, Agha Sahab loves Hassan equally to his son Amir. He treats both equally. He does not love Amir more than Hassan although Hassan is a servant. This thing plays a role of the snare in which suspense is created by avoiding the truth. "If changed my mind and asked for a bigger and fancier kite. Baba would buy it for me but then he'd buy it for Hassan too, Sometimes I wished he wouldn't do that. Wished he'd let me be the favorite" (Hosseini, p. 48). These lines reflect the love of Agha for Hassan. If Amir wants a bigger kite, Agha buys two one for Amir and one for Hassan. This shows the deep love of Agha for Hassan too. Agha treats Hassan as his son. This unusual love works as a snare. The truth behind love is avoided in the initial part of the novel. This snare is untied in the last part of the novel.

On the birthday of Hassan, Baba gives a special gift which creates tension in the mind of Aamir about Baba's abnormal favors to Hassan. Baba arranges a surgeon to fix the cleft lip of Hassan. The researcher finds enigma in the behavior of Baba for Hassan. Amir is jealous that Baba would do so much for Hassan. The surgery is a success, and by the next winter, Hassan's cleft lip is just a faint scar.

Winter is considered the best time for Kabul because everyone takes part in kite flying tournaments. There is a war among boy about kites. Everyone prepares special strings to cut the kites of their opponents. Amir knows that Hassan is the best kite runner in the whole of Kabul. Baba wishes Amir to win the kite-fighting tournament. Amir is excited to make Baba happy by winning the tournament. Hassan tells Amir about his last night dream and their swimming in the Ghargha Lake. They rename the lake "Lake of Amir and Hassan, Sultans of Kabul" (Hosseini, P. 87). Amir is so nervous that he almost wants to quit the tournament, but Hassan reminds him that "there's no monster," and Amir is again amazed at Hassan's intuition" (Hosseini, P. 60). After a long battle of the kite, Amir manages to cut the last blue kite. Amir and Hassan are happy. Hassan promises to run the kite for Amir, he says "for you a thousand times over!" (Hosseini P. 67).

Later on, Amir runs to find the Hassan. He searches everywhere and finally finds him in an alley, holding the blue kite which Amir thinks of as the "key to Baba's heart" (Hosseini P.71). Assef offers Hassan freedom on dropping of the blue kite but Hassan is not ready for this. Assef reminds him that he is only a servant of Amir. Assef and company forces Hassan for rape. Amir watching from the corner and the words of Ali are echoing in his ears, "there is a brotherhood between people who've fed from the same breast" (Hosseini P.73). Amir watches cowardly when Hassen is raped by Assef in the alley. Amir sacrifices Hassan for the blue kite to make Baba happy.

This code also refers as Delay. In this code, things are delayed to make the reader more curious about the situation. In chapter 7, Hassan is raped and Amir sees all the incident. Although Amir knows the reality he pretends that he knows nothing. He acts as he is very concerned with Hassan. As Amir says "Where were you? I looked for you," I said. Speaking those words was like chewing on a rock" (Hosseini, p. 73). In this line, Amir interrogates Hassan about his absence although he knows about the inhumane happening. He pretends to be fretful about Hassan by saying that he searches for him. Amir also elaborates that the utterance of these words seems to like to chew stones and rocks. The behavior of Amir generates the query, why does Amir hide the reality and act fake in front of Hassan? Why does he not take stand for Hassan? Why does Amir not console Hassan? These questions generate in the mind of a reader but answers are delayed to make the reader more interested in the novel.

After that their friendship, their smooth and happy relations turns into guilt and bad memories. When Amir turns thirteen Baba decides to throw him a huge party. Baba invites around 400 people. Assef also arrives and gives Amir a gift, a biography of Hitler. From the story of Rahim Khan, Amir gets the idea to get rid of Hassan. Amir designs a plan, he hides some of the money and his watch under Hassan's mattress. And then he told Baba about the theft. Baba calls everyone and tries to settle the matter. Baba asks Hassan bout the theft and Hassan says he did.

Delay is also a technique which is used in the Hermeneutic code of Barthes. This term suspends the answers to particular questions which build in the mind of the reader. In the novel when Amir accuses Hassan of the theft because theft is only one sin which is unforgivable by Agha Jan. The reader is in the suspense when this sin is forgiven by Agha Jan. "Except Baba stunned me by saying, "I forgive you." *Forgive*? But theft was the one unforgivable sin, the common denominator of all sins" (Hosseini, p. 98). "Then how could he just forgive Hassan? And if baba could forgive that, then why couldn't he forgive me for not being the son he'd always wanted? (Hosseini, p. 98)". These lines express that Agha Jan forgives Hassan on the sin of theft. This forgiveness is shocking for Amir. The narrator himself raises the questions which are taken place in the mind of the reader. The answers are delayed deliberately by Hosseini to maintain the interest of the reader. The questions take place, why does Agha Jan forgive Hassan's sin? Why cannot Agha Jan forgive Amir on not being a son as he like? These suspended answers create inclination of the reader to resolve.

The narrative jumps to March of 1981. Baba with Amir leaves Afghanistan to Pakistan and from thence to America. Afghanistan is under the control of Russain soldiers. Everyone is suspicious of everyone around. Anybody can inform for money. Karim first takes them to Jalalabad, then in a fuel tanker to Peshawar. Every check post has some danger for them because the Russain soldier is everywhere. At one post, a Russian soldier demands a young woman as a price to pass them. Baba stands for them and soldier threatens to shoot him. Just before the Russian soldier decides another soldier interrupts him.

The narrative skips in time and Baba and Amir live in Freemont, California for almost two years. Baba is facing a hard time to adjust to the new environment. Amir graduates from high school at the age of twenty and Baba feels pride at the success of Amir. Next Sunday Amir sets a booth at a flea market and sells for a profit. Amir is introduced to General Taheri and his beautiful daughter, Soraya. Amir falls in love with Soraya. But there are rumors about her past loss of honor. A full year passes to collect the nerve to talk to her. But Baba understands what is going on inside his son. Amir often manages to talk to her when her father is away. Sorry reveals that she wants to be a teacher. When Amir gives Soraya his story to read, the General throws the story in the trash. Another obstacle to Amir's love story comes when Baba gets the sickness. The doctors want to give chemotherapy but Baba denies. Baba grows weaker day by day. He loses a lot of weight. One day he even collapsed on the ground. The cancer spreads to the brain of Baba. After getting better, Baba asks General Taheri for the marriage of Amir and Soraya and he approves. Before marriage, Soraya tells her past story of elopement and exposes her troubled past to Amir. Amir envies her because he has no courage to reveal his troubled past.

In the summer of 1988, Amir's first novel is published and he becomes a celebrity in the Afghan community. Ultimately he achieves his dream of becoming the writer.

Amir and Soraya try to have a baby but fails. They are thinking to adopt a child. In June of 2001, Amir receives a call from Rahim Khan, who wants Amir to come and see him. He suggests that there is still a way to be good again. It is also exposed that Rahim Khan knows about the alley incident. Amir visits Pakistan and then from there he goes to Afghanistan. Everything reminds him of the past.

Rahim Khan tells Amir about the past incidents and accidents happened in Afghanistan. After Soviets left, different groups took over different parts of Kabul. And violence becomes a daily routine. Bab's orphanage had been destroyed. He further tells about Hassan and his wife, Farzana. He tells that Ali had been killed by a land mine. Hassan names his son after Sohrab, a character from Rosam and Sohrab story. In 1996 however, the Taliban took over the country and they banned kit fighting. Taliban massacred the Hazara community of Mazar e Sharif. One day Taliban enter into the house of Baba and they capture Hassan as a Hazarah. They made Hassan kneel before them and finally shot him in the back of his head. Farzana is also killed by the Taliban. Then they capture the Baba's house and they sent Sohrab to an orphanage.

Rahim Khan tells Amir that the main purpose of his return is to save Sohrab. Rahim Khan reminds Amir about his need to face the difficulties. It is also disclosed that Hassan is actually his real brother. Rahim Khan shows him a way to end the cycle of betrayals and lies. Amir wears a fake beard which reaches to his chest because a requirement in the Taliban occupied areas. In Kabul Amir does not recognize the alleys and houses as everything has been turned into rubbles. Even teachers are turned into beggars. He is told that Sohrab is taken by a Taliban in an orphanage. That Taliban official turns out Assef, an old enemy of Amir. Assef says that he is on a mission to clean Afghanistan from all types of garbage. Assef wears his old brass knuckles and beat Amir badly. He bleeds. Assef then throws him against the wall and strikes him hard. But Amir starts laughing. He suddenly feels peace and calmness in his heart. He feels healed not broken. Sohrab loads his slingshot and hit at the Assef's eye. Assef screams and rolls around on the floor. Amir and Sohrab run and escape to Peshawar.

Sohrab barely speaks to anybody. They paly panjpar in silence. Amir decides to take Sohrab to Islamabad. Amir promise to Sohrab that he will not send Sohrab to an orphanage then Sohrab agrees to go to America. Then the problem of no death certificate of

Sohrab's parents. Next day they meet Faisal, the lawyer, who says that it is difficult but not impossible. Faisal opines that they have to put Sohrab in an orphanage for two years at least. Sohrab out of distress tries to commit suicide. Amir turns to God for help and realizes that there is no hope except God. With the help of Soraya relatives, they manage to migrate to America with Sohrab.

The hermeneutic code deals with mystery and suspense. In the novel, the residence in America is suspense for the readers. The suspense is originated that whether they will live here forever or leave the place. "For me, America was a place to bury my memories. For Baba, a place to mourn his" (Hosseini, p. 120). This line elucidates the paradoxical feelings of Amir and Agha Jan. Amir finds solace in America whereas Agha Jan mourns there. These contradictory feelings generate the question that will they live in America or leave it one day? The mystery is resolved by the readers in further episodes.

The puzzle is created when Rahim Khan tells about Hassan. "You know all those years I lived in your father's house after you left? "I wasn't alone for all of them. Hassan lived there with me"(Hosseini, p. 186). In these lines, Rahim Khan tells Amir that he and Hassan live in their house for many years. This develops the puzzle in the novel that why does Hassan return to the house? This is shocking for Amir and the readers. This unexpected and mysterious element maintains the uncertainty in the novel.

The mystery is developed in chapter number 17 when there is a tussle between Rahim and Amir. Rahim wants Amir to help Sohrab and Amir does not want to help Sohrab. "Children are fragile, Amir Jan. Kabul is already full of broken children and I don't want Sohrab to become another one." "Rahim Khan, I don't want to go Kabul. I can't!" I said. "Sohrab is a gifted little boy. We can give him a new life here, new hope, with people who would love him" (Hosseini, p. 204). These lines indicate that Amir is not willing to help Sohrab. Rahim Khan tries to convince Amir to give Sohraba better life. Amir does not want to go Kabul as Kabul is a dangerous place. The scrimmage between Amir and Rahim on the subject of Sohrabendures the suspense. Will Amir help Sohrab or not? Will he give a new life to Sohrabor not?

The hermeneutic code also helps to unveil the mysterious elements in the novel. The mystery of the love of Agha for Hassan is resolved when Rahim Khan convinces Amir for the life of Sohrab. The mystery is revealed on Amir and on the readers as well.

"No, he wasn't. He and Sanaubar had Hassan, didn't they? They had Hassan.

No, they didn't, Rahim Khan said.

Yes, they did!

No, they didn't, Amir.

Then Who

I think you know who" (Hosseini, P. 205-206).

In these lines the suspense of the real relationship between Amir, Hassan and Agha are disclosed as Amir says that Hassan is the son of Ali and Sanaubar. On the other hand, Rahim Khan indirectly exposes that Hassan is not the son of Ali but he is half-brother to Amir. The suspense is unveiled through readers.

The resolution of one suspense creates another suspense in the story. In the novel the mystery that whether Amir helps Sohrab or nor is resolved but generates another mystery."Then I told him I was going to Kabul. Told him to call the Caldwells in the morning. "I'll pray for you, Amir Jan," he said" (Hosseini, p.210). These lines elucidate that Amir is agreed to help Sohrab. On this, another suspense is created that whether Amir will be successful to give Sohraba new life or he will face failure. Hermeneutic code rises questions and unveils the suspense through these queries.

Amir finds an Afghan kite seller and buys a kite, and he takes it over to Sohrab. Amir checks the string and talks to Sohrab about Hassan and his skill at kite-flying and kite-running. Amir asks if Sohrabwants to fly the kite, but there is no response. Amir starts running, the kite rising behind him, and then he realizes Sohrabis following him. Amir feels a rush of joy, as he hasn't flown a kite in decades. Amir offers again, and Sohrabhesitantly takes the kite string. Amir wishes time would stand still. Then a green kite approaches for a fight and Sohrab hands the spool back to Amir, but he looks alert and alive, interested in the kites. Amir shows Sohrabwhat was Hassan's favorite trick, and soon they have trapped the green kite, with Amir flying and Sohrabholding the spool. Amir lets himself slip into his memories of Kabul, Hassan, Ali, and Baba, and then he cuts the string of the green kite. Behind them, people cheer for their victory, and the tiniest smile appears on Sohrab's face. Amir knows it is only a little thing, but it is perhaps a sign of better things to come, an omen of hope for the future. Amir asks if he should run the green kite for Sohrab, and Sohrabnods. Amir says "for you, a thousand times over," and he sets off running with a smile on his face.

4.2.3. Conclusion

The present chapter studies the Hermeneutic code of Barthes in Hosseini's masterpiece. Roland Barthes has claimed that every text can be analyzed through the lenses of five codes theory. The codes are followings "Hermeneutic code", "Proairetic code", "Symbolic code", "Cultural code" and "Semantic code". This chapter analyzes the text through the code of enigma. The Hermeneutic code also called the "voice of truth". It deals with mysterious elements in the text. The code argues that elements which create suspense formulate the plot of the novel. The paper finds out that the suspense among people, in conversations and in actions develops the interest of readers in the novel.

4.3   An Exploration of Symbolic Code (SEM)

This chapter explores the structure of the novel *The Kite Runner* by Khaled Hosseini. This chapter is about to investigate the way in which the dialectic system conveys meanings. In structuralism, a system is always involved in the propagation of meanings. It elaborates that meanings of an entity are determined by its opposite entity. No single word can stand alone without its antonym in a system. The purpose of this chapter is to find binary oppositions and antithetic codes in the novel *The Kite Runner*. The research aims at an understanding of the role of antonyms to accommodate Hosseini for forming the text of *The Kite Runner*. In order to analyze the text, the researcher applies Roland Barthes' concept of Symbolic Code with the help of Levis Straus' Binary Oppositions. Roland Barthes propounds the idea of Symbolic Code in his book *S/Z*. Barthes introduces symbolic code which refers to the antithetic code. In Barthes' view of identifying a word, an entity or thought, it is necessary to study its opposite word, entity or thought. Similarly, Claude Lewis Straus also proposes the same idea that through the system of binary meanings are derived. One sign is recognized by its opposite sign. Straus claims that the human brain is language structured and language is a binary system. He argues just as words are based on contrast, human thoughts are also based on contrast to derive meanings. The findings of this research suggest that the structure of Hosseini's novel *The Kite Runner* is constructed out of binaries and dialectic codes. The implication of this research is to recommend the comprehension of opposite ideas for understanding, identifying distinguishing and determining the meanings of two words, ideas or entities.

To conduct the study, textual evidence is collected to explore and analyze the significance of binary opposition and symbolic code in the novel, *The Kite Runner*. This research is qualitative in its nature. This research is inductive and fundamental since it deals with the theoretical understanding rather practical solution of something concrete. For the analysis of the text, the guiding principles have been taken from Roland Barthes' theory of *Five Codes*. Roland Gerard Barthes was a French literary theorist, philosopher, linguist, critic, and semiotician. He was born on 12 November 1915 and died on 26 March 1980. Barthes' ideas explored a diverse range of fields and he influenced the development of schools of theory including Structuralism, Semiotics, Social Theory, and Post-Structuralism. In his book, *S/Z* (Barthes, 1970) described and demonstrated methods of literary analysis. He while analyzing Balzac's story 'Sarrasine' identified Five Codes. By propagating this theory, Barthes claims that every story contains the Five Codes i.e. hermeneutic code, Proairetic code, semantic code, symbolic code, and cultural code. In the current research, the researcher focuses on one codenamed as a symbolic code. In Barthes' view of identifying a word, an entity or thought, it is necessary to study its opposite word, entity or thought. Roland Barthes argues that one idea is always understood through its opposite idea or thought. In the book *S/Z*, Barthes propounds symbolic code in which he suggests that transgression, replication of bodies and antithetic codes help readers to internalize the specific concept.

In order to support Barthes' concept of symbolic code second theory which is going to be applied has been taken from Levis Straus' model of Binary Oppositions. Claude Levis Straus was born in 1908 and died in 2009. He was social structuralist. He argues society depends on the structure which is definitely based on Binary Oppositions.

4.3.1. Textual Analysis

'Within novels, the symbolic code is commonly used as a polemic to present the superiority of one idea over another. Scholarly writers sometimes take this literary motif to the extreme by employing binary opposites on the literary and abstract levels in tandem' (Klages, 2006). This internally-reinforced structure serves the author's purpose by providing the reader with several noticeable archetypes on the literary level that are inextricably linked with a thematic binary-pair that is embedded at the abstract level. Several writers use this technique to give meanings their written words and to confirm the prestige of one idea over others. For instance, Edger Allen Poe, in his gothic stories, applies this code extensively. David Shane exclaims: "The binary pair that Poe uses, in his story *The Cask of Amontillado,* is the name of characters. The protagonist's name is "Fortunato" which means "fortunate, happy, blessed, and Poe indirectly supplies the Montresor family, representation of serpent" (Shane, 2015, p.2).

Roland Barthes argues that one idea is always understood through its opposite idea or thought. In the book *S/Z,* Barthes propounds symbolic code in which he suggests that transgression, replication of bodies and antithetic codes help readers to internalize the specific concept. Critic Barry explains:

"Symbolic code is also termed as the antithetic code. The code is somehow like the semantic code but its function is deeper than the latter one. It refers to those elements that give opposite meanings, i.e. have polarities and antithesis. The concept of polarities or binary oppositions is central to the theory of Structuralism. By these binary oppositions, a structuralist understands reality." (Barry, 2002, p.151).

At the start of the novel, Amir is thirty-eight, who lives in California. Amir receives a phone call from Rahim Khan, who asks if Amir can visit him. He is calling from Pakistan. He tells Amir he knows of "a way to be good again"(Hosseinie, 2013, p. 02). The call brings memories of the past, 1975. He remembers the kite runner Hassan who was his childhood playmate, servant, and antithesis.

There are binaries and replication e.g Hassan is the son of Ali, who is a servant of Baba. Amir's father was a wealthy man who owned the most beautiful house in the Wazir Akbar Khan, District of Kabul. Amir's mother died during childbirth and Hassan's deserted him when he was only five days old. The same woman nursed both the boys. Further, Hassan is of Hazara while Amir is Pashtun. They are minority ethnically and religious wise. Hassan and Ali are Shia's Muslim and Amir and Baba are Suni's Muslim. Hassan lives in a mud hut behind the big house of Amir. Amir's father was a physically strong person rather Ali is partially paralyzed. Amir does not like sports and he refuses to stand up for himself against bullies rather he reads books and write stories. Hassan always fights against bullies and often defends Amir. Amir was selfish and feels the inability to give any sacrifice. Hassan always sacrifices   for   the   sake   of   Amir.

when Amir writes a story about a man whose tears turned into

pearls, he was not appreciated by Baba. But Rahim Khan asks him

to read the story and he writes a note of appreciation for Amir

in the transition of the political scenario is mentioned when it is

written that Zahir Shah was overthrown by his cousin Daud Khan.

The Soviet Union take over Afghanistan in December of 1979.

it shows the end of one era and the start of another era. Binaries of

time   are   mentioned   here.

Before the war and bloodshed, there was a different Afghanistan.

Where Winter meant the start of kite flying and fighting season.

Kabul was a place where boys play kite fighting games. The glass

strings are used to fly kites which allow the flyer to cut the other's

string.

Amir was the kite flyer and Hassan was the kite runner. He had an

internal sense about the kites. He knows where the kite is going to

land after it had been cut loose from its flyer. Even amir was

jealous of Hassan's ability to run quickly. Baba spent much more

time on Hassan's kite than Amir's. Baba expects Amir to win the largest tournament of kite fighting. Amir knew that his father takes him as a failure. So he thought a win would change this attitude. there were forty-eight kites in the tournament but Amir kept fighting and gradually cutting out his competitors until his fight with a blue kite. Finally, he managed to cut the last blue kite too, which made him the sole winner of the kite-fighting tournament. Baba was very happy. It was one of the greatest moments of Amir's life. Baba wanted the blue kite. Hassan ran for it. Amir ran behind Hassan and he saw Hassan being confronted by Assef and company. The blue kite is demanded by the bullies but Hassan is not ready to give that. Assef allowed him to keep the kite but at a certain price. Hassan was sodomized by Assef and company. Amir did not muster his courage to face the bullies. He was afraid of Assef and company. in 1976, his father celebrated his thirteenth birthday and threw a lavish party. Asef gave a biography of Hitler as a gift and Hassan gave Shahnama as a birthday gift. Their birthday gifts signify their bent of minds. Two different antithetical attitudes. Amir decided to get rid of Hassan and his father as they were reminding of his guilt for not stopping Hassan's rape. He planned and ensured that his father would never forgive theft. Hassan admitted the theft of the items and Baba forgave him, much to his surprise.

five years later in 1981, Baba and Amir were leaving Afghanistan due to Soviet invasion. the time of harmony, peace, kite flying is over. The time of war, fight, bloodshed, and torment are started. from Pakistan, they left for America. Baba, in California, worked at a gas station for a living. He did not like California. Amir's career choice initially dismayed Baba but eventually, he accepted it. at a flea market, Amir has introduced the beautiful Soraya with whom he was instantly in love. they are married and lived in California when Amir receives a phone call from Rahim Khan. Last words beforehand up were, "Come, There is a way to be good again" (Hosseinie, 2013, p.226). After a week of call, Amir was on his way to Pakistan. Rahim told about the past events to Amir. After Soviet Taliban moved in with their own form of violence. Rahim told that he brought Hassan back to live in the house again. who came with his pregnant wife, Farzana. On the other hand, it is told that Soyara was struggling to get pregnant. Farzana gave birth to a stillborn baby girl and then in 1990 she again got pregnancy. Hassan's mother Sanaubar came back to him. In that winter Sanauber served as a midwife to Hassan's child, Sohrab.

In 1996, the Taliban banned the kite fighting in Kabul. They killed a lot of Hazara on the basis of sectarian difference. One day they found Hassan living in Baba's house, the Taliban dragged him in the street and eventually shot him and his wife Farzana. Now Rahim Khan wants Amir to go to Kabul and bring young Sohrab back. Amir who was always afraid to make any dangerous journey. Rahim khan exposed the secret that Hassan's true father was Baba. Finally, Amir decided to visit Afghanistan and brought back Sohrab.

once beautiful city was now turned into ditch.there was no water or electricity. The streets were full of waste and rubbles. Beggars were everywhere in the streets. Even a former university professor was turned into a begger, who also knew his mother. The sports stadium was being used for stoning to death. Now Assef held Sohrab for his personal entertainment. He makes the boy dance for him. Assef was proud of his acts of murder in the people in the name of God. He abused the children of the orphanage. He even took his brass knuckles to beat Amir. But the boy hit Assef's eye by his father's slingshot. Then they escaped to Pakistan. Finally, Amir found his courage to face the danger. Islamabad was a clean and beautiful city but Afghanistan was turned into a battlefield.

Khaled Hosseini in his novel, *The Kite Runner* focuses on the antithetic codes and creates a number of binary pairs like those of geographical binaries, emotional binaries, relational binaries, verbal binaries, seasonal binaries, religious binaries, character lead binaries, racial binaries and binary of beauty vs ugliness.

4.3.1.2. Geographical binaries:

In the novel, The Kite Runner, there are geographical binaries. Hosseini divides the plot of the novel into different regions. This special distinction among different countries makes an ideology that life gets changed into its dimensions through the change in geographical settings. With reference to his characters, Hosseini describes many regions like those of Hassan belongs to Hazara, Amir belongs to Kabul and Rahim Khan belongs to Pakistan.

Kabul	Hazara
"We took strolls in the bazaars of the Shar-e-Nau section of *Kabul* in the west of the Wazir Akbar Khan district" (Hosseini, 2013, p.25).	"You! The *Hazara*! Look at me when I'm talking to you!" (Hosseini, 2013, p.7). "They called him flat nosed because of Ali and Hassan's characteristic *Hazara* Mongoloid features" (Hosseini, 2013, p.8).
Afghanistan	**Pakistan**
"The year Zahir Shah began his forty-year reign of *Afghanistan* (Hosseini, 2013, p.23).	"One-day last summer, my friend Rahim Khan called from *Pakistan*" (Hosseini, 2013, p.1).
Jalalabad	**California**
"Karim's cousin was here in *Jalalabad* and could probably fit	"Padat moved us to *California*"

us all" (Hosseini, 2013, p.112).	(Hosseini, 2013, p.151).
Russia "Fuck the *Russia*" (Hosseini, 2013, p.123)	**America** "For me, *America* was a place to bury my memories" (Hosseini, 2013, p.120).
German "Assefsnickered. He sounds like my mother and she's *German*" (Hosseini, 2013, p. 37). "Born to a *German* mother and Afghan father, the blond, blue-eyed Asseftowered over the other kids" (Hosseini, 2013, p.35).	**Italy** "The King, Zahir Shah, was away in *Italy*. In his absence, his cousin Daoud Khan had ended the King's forty-year reign" (Hosseini, 2013, p.34).
Wazir Akbar Khan "Baba had built the most	**Virginia** "Soraya said. When we lived in

beautiful house in the *Wazir Khan district*, in the northern part of Kabul" (Hosseini, 2013, p.4)	*Virginia*, I became ESL certified" (Hosseini, 2013, p.139).
China "I can see Hassan's perfectly round face, a face like a *Chinese* doll" (Hosseini, 2013, p.3).	**Japan** "He bought him a *Japanese* toy truck one year, an electric locomotive and train track set another year" (Hosseini, 2013, p.41).
Golden Gate Park "I went for a walk along Spreckels Lake on the northern edge of *Golden Gate Park*" (Hosseini, 2013, p.1).	**Park in Fremont** "I remember the two of us walking through Lake Elizabeth *Park in Fremont*" (Hosseini, 2013, p.116).

Zarghoona High School in Kabul	Ohlone Junior College in Fremont
"My mother was a teacher too, she taught Farsi and history at *Zarghoona High School for girls in Kabul*" (Hosseini, 2013, p.139).	"Soraya was telling about her general education classes, at *Ohlone Junior College in Fremont*" (Hosseini, 2013, p.139).
Kandahar	**Peshawar**
"*Kandahar* at once and enlist in the army for one year" (Hosseini, 2013, p.23).	"Then we'd be on our way to *Peshawar*. On to freedom. On to safety" (Hosseini, 2013, p.110).

4.3.1.2 Emotional Binaries:

In emotional binaries, one mental state is often privileged over others. Emotions play a crucial role in the determination of an individual's personality. Laughter and tears are two dissimilar mental conditions. Laughter most often symbolizes happiness, satisfaction, and confidence, but on the other hand, tear represents sadness, grief, pain, and precarious mental condition. Khaled Hosseini, in his novel, *The Kite Runner*, makes a comparison between two opposite emotional guts like those of love and hatred, happiness and sadness, laughter and tears, and patience and impatience. In Barthes' views, one symbolic code gives the recognition of others (Barthes, 1970). Similarly, Claude Levis Strauss theorizes that "comparison may help us to explain what we have in mind" (Strauss, 2015). So, in order to make readers understand the difference between emotions, Hosseini makes a comparison between two distinctive mental statuses.

Happiness	Sadness
Happiness is a mental state in which one feels pleasure and satisfied. Hosseini uses physical laughter as a tool to represent the mental recreational	Opposite to happiness, sadness is the representation of mental captivity and disorder. Dialectically, Hosseini applies the technique of tears and

enthusiasm of his characters. As in the text: "One of the yellow-haired tourists *laughed* and slapped the other one on the back" (Hosseini, 2013, p.14). "I *laughed*. Clutched him in a hug and planted a kiss on his cheek" (Hosseini, 2013, p.29).	sobbing (opposite to laughter) in order to show the sadness of his characters. "Hassan dragged a sleeve across his face, wiped snot and *tears*" (Hosseini, 2013, p.73). "He *cried*. It scared me a little, seeing a grown man *sob*" (Hosseini, 2013, p.100).
Love	**Hatred**
"The man is Pashtun to the root. He has *nang and namoos*. Nang and namoos. Honor and Pride" (Hosseini, 2013, p.134). Agha Sahib's statement indicates his love for	"*Fuck* the Russia" (Hosseini, 2013, p.122). Baba's aggressive utterance shows his mental and emotional pain which he gets from the Russian invasion of Afghanistan.

Afghanistan and Pashtuns. "I love wintertime in Kabul" (Hosseini, 2013, p.46).	
Patience	**Impatience**
Aamir has patience. Whenever he speaks and performs some action, Aamir exhibits tolerance in his behavior. "Farid, *sit down! Let it go!* I said" (Hosseini, 2013, p.236).	Opposite to Aamir, Hosseini portrays another character named Farid who represents impatience in his behavior. "Farid was leaping over the table. Zaman's chair went flying as *Farid fell on him and pinned him* to the floor" (Hosseini, 2013, p.236). "

4.3.1.3. Relational Binaries

Grandfather and grandson

1.1 Aamir and his grandfather:

"A thief walked into *my grandfather's* house. *My grandfather*, a respected judge, confronted him, but the thief stabbed" (Hosseini, 2013, p.17).

Father and Son

1.2 Aamir and Agha Sahib:

"Everyone agreed that *my father, my Baba*, had built the most beautiful house" (Hosseini, 2013, p.4).

"I was glad to because then everyone would see that he was *my father, my Baba*" (Hosseini, 2013, p.14).

1.3 Hassan and Ali:

"Father! What's that sound? Hassan yelped, his hands outstretched toward *Ali*" (Hosseini, 2013, p.33).

1.4 Assefand Mehmood:

"Assef was the *son* of one of my father's friend, *Mehmood,* an airline pilot" (Hosseini, 2013, p.35).

1.5 Kamal and Father:

"I discovered that two of the people hiding with us were *Kamal and his father*" (Hosseini, 2013, p.111).

Father and Daughter

1.6 General Taheri and Soraya Jan:

"*My daughter*, Soraya Jan, Dr. Taheri said" (Hosseini, 2013, p.130).

Mother and Son

1.7 Hassan and Sanaubar:

"Hassan's *mother Sanaubar* gave birth to him one cold winter day in 1964" (Hosseini, 2013, p.6)

1.8 Aamir and Sofia:

"He wedded *my mother*, Sofia Akrami" (Hosseini, 2013, p.15).

1.9 Assefand Mother:

"Assefwas born to a *German mother* and Afghan father" (Hosseini, 2013, p.35).

Mother and Daughter

1.10 Soraya and Jamila:

"I am Jamila, *Soraya Jan's mother*" (Hosseini, 2013, p.136).

Owner and Servant

1.11 Aamir and Hassan:

"He is not my friend. He is my *servant*" (Hosseini, 2013, p.38).

Husband and Wife

1.12 Agha Sahib and Sofia:

"He *wedded my mother*, Sofia Akrami" (Hosseini, 2013, p.15).

"Baba said, his *wife's* right to her *husband*" (Hosseini, 2013, p.17).

"They stuck and killed a Hazara *husband* and a *wife* on a road"

(Hosseini, 2013, p.23).

1.13 Mr. and Mrs. Nguyen:

"A little grocery store run by an elderly Vietnamese, *Mr. and Mrs. Nguyen*" (Hosseini, 2013, p.118).

4.3. 1.4. Religious Binaries

By giving the religious binaries in the novel *The Kite Runner*, Hosseini highlights the sectarian and religious conflicts among Muslims in Afghanistan. In Afghanistan especially in Kabul Sunni Pashtuns are regarded over the Hazara Shias.

Sunni	Shi'a

"Pashtuns had opposed the Hazaras was that Pashtuns were *Sunni* Muslims, while Hazaras were *Shi'a*" (Hosseini, 2013, p.9).	"I was Pashtun and he was a Hazara, I was *Sunni* and he was *Shi'a*" (Hosseini, 2013, p.24).

4.3.1.5 Seasonal binaries

Seasonal binaries are too present in the novel *The Kite Runner* by Khaled Hosseini.

Summer	Winter
"One-day last *summer*, my friend Rahim Khan called from Pakistan" (Hosseini, 2013, p.1).	"So every *winter* Baba picked something out himself" (Hosseini, 2013, p.41).
Spring	**Autumn**
"One Sunday in the *spring* of 1983, I walked into a small	"Seasons of *rain and snow* had turned the iron gate rusty"

bookstore" (Hosseini, 2013, p.119).	(Hosseini, 2013, p.26).

4.3.1.6. Verbal Binaries

Claude Levis Straus argues that the human mind is language structured. In language, one lexeme exists because of its opposite lexeme and even one sound gives meanings on the behalf of its antonyms. A is 'A' because there is 'B'. The researcher has found verbal binaries in the text entitled *The Kite Runner* by Khaled Hosseini.

Sleeping	Awaking
"Ali and Hassan were *sleeping* on a mattress" (Hosseini, 2013, p.31).	"I shook Hassan *awake* and asked him if he wanted to hear a story" (Hosseini, 2013, p.31).
Gone	Live
"The *king* is gone" (Hosseini,	"Long *live* the president"

2013, p.37).	(Hosseini, 2013, p.37).
Subside	**Heal**
"The swelling *subsided*" (Hosseini, 2013, p.44).	"The wound *healed*" (Hosseini, 2013, p.44).

4.4. Conclusion

The chapter has been planned to investigate the idea of antithetic code and binary opposition in the novel, *The Kite Runner* by Khaled Hosseini, an Afghan fiction writer and currently living in America in the perspective of Roland Barthes' concept of symbolic code with the help of Claude Levis Strauss' theory of binary opposition. This chapter also aims at an understanding of the role of binary opposition in the determination of meanings. In the novel, *The Kite Runner*, the researcher emphasizes six kinds of binaries which include: geographical, emotional, relational, religious, seasonal, and verbal. Roland Barthes propounds the idea of Symbolic Code in his book *S/Z*. Barthes introduces symbolic code which refers to the antithetic code. In Barthes' view of identifying a word, an entity or thought it is necessary to study its opposite word, entity or thought. Similarly, Claude Lewis Straus also proposes the same idea that through the system of binary meanings are derived. One sign is recognized by its opposite sign. Straus claims that the human brain is language structured and language is a binary system. He argues just as words are based on contrast, human thoughts are also based on contrast to derive meanings. The findings of this research suggest that the structure of Hosseini's novel *The Kite Runner* is constructed out of binaries and dialectic codes.

4.4 An Exploration Of Semantic Code (SEM)

The present chapter analyzes the novel *The kite runner* under the light of the voice of a person, Semantic code. The study is significant as it paves the way for other researchers to study a text through a Barthesian code. Barthes has given the five codes of narrative in his book *S/Z*. This chapter studies the novel under the Semantic code, the voice of a person, any element in a text that suggests a particular and additional meaning by way of connotation. This code helps to build up 'the quality and depth of a character or an action' and understand 'the dominant motifs of personal characters'. Semantic code is vital to give soul to the story. The soul of a text is the theme and the readers can draw out themes through connotative meaning.

4.4.1.Data Analysis

The opening of the novel suggests that history and memory will play an important role in the text. Some past event still haunts the mind of Amir and he is looking to "be good again"– to redeem himself somehow (Hosseinie, 2013, p.01). Kites suggest past guilt and symbolize hope. The story then unfolds back in time. it is unfolded that Amir and Hassan were inseparable once. Semi code suggests the elements in the novel which are comprehended by the suggestive meanings. Semi code refers to abnormal and exaggerated things in the text which covey additional meanings. This code forms themes in the novel. The novel *The Kite Runner* deals with connotative meanings and exaggerated elements which provide the soul to the novel. In the novel, the physical appearance of Hassan is described in an unusual way. The narrator of the novel uses astonishing and farfetched images for the features of Hassan.

Round face, a face like a Chinese doll chiseled from hardwood leaves, eyes that looked, depending on the light, gold, green, even sapphire. I can still see his tiny low-set ears and that pointed stub of a chin, a meaty appendage that looked like it was added as a mere afterthought. And the cleft lip, just left of midline, where the Chinese doll maker's instrument may have slipped, or perhaps he had simply grown tired and careless (Hosseini, p. 3)

These lines suggest the semi code plays an important role in the formation of the text. As in chapter number 2, the narrator describes Hassan as a Chinese doll. The narrator portrays Hassan as Chinese doll made up of "hardwood leaves". His eyes depend on the light of green, gold stones. His ears are small and chin is stubbed. His lip is split. It seems that he is a defected piece of a doll maker. Hassan looks like a careless production of a Chinese doll maker. The unusual ugly representation of Hassan in the novel suggests that Hassan is considered as for granted and mediocre creature. His physical appearance reflects his value in the society of Pashtuns. Hassan's below the average appearance shows his lower status in the surrounding.

Khaled Hosseini gives voice to the oppressed class of the society. He promoted a discourse which highlights the abject condition of the Hazara community in Kabul. Ali, father of Hassan lives a drastic life. He is described as half paralyzed which symbolizes his paralyzed social status in Afghanistan.

The character of the Baba is presented as larger than life figure, who has spent his life fighting with bear-like things. He has achieved many successes in his life

Semi code also helps to build the quality of the character. This code refers to dig out the depth of action and character through the use of exaggerated and odd images. In the novel, the character of Agha Jan is depicted in an unusual way. Agha Jan's persona represents his inner personality and his status in the society in which he lives. "Hands that looked capable of uprooting a willow tree, and a black glare that would "drop the devil to his knees begging for mercy" as Rahim Khan used to say. At parties, when all six-foot-five of him thundered into the room attention shifted to him like sunflowers turning to the sun"(Hosseini, p. 13). In these lines, Agha Jan's hands are compared with the willow tree. Willow tree refers to as protection. The hands of Agha suggests protection. His black gaze can drop the devil to knees for the appeal of pity. His black eyes represent the strong and brave glare that can frighten the evil. Moreover, Rahim Khan praises Agha and uses a metaphor of the sun for him. He elaborates that in functions people's attention shift to him as flowers turn to the sun for energy. It suggests that Agha Jan provide energy and liveliness to people.

Khaled Hosseini paints the moving social picture of the time when he describes the social divide between conservative, fundamentalist Muslims like Amir's teacher and liberal Afghans like Baba in the text. When in the form of Taliban they take over the government and power they spread terror and violence in the society.

Semantic code transactions with the connotative meanings that give understanding to the readers. It gives help to draw themes from the text. In the novel, the binary of Hazara and Pashtun give the theme of racism in Afghanistan. "Never mind any of those things. Because history isn't easy to overcome. Neither is religion. In the end, I was a Pashtun and he was a Hazara. I was Sunni and he was Shia, and nothing was ever going to change that. Nothing" (Hosseini, p. 24). These lines elucidate that history and religion play an important role to inculcate thoughts in the mind of people. Amir says in that religion and history cannot be controlled. These both control people. Amir is Sunni and Hassan is Shia. They are categorized by history and religion. In the perspective of history, Amir is Pashtun and Hassan is Hazara. In the perspective of religion, Amir is Sunni and Hassan is Shia. This code helps to understand the theme of racism and prejudice. The division of sects, religion, and territory give the theme of racial discrimination and prejudice.

This code makes the reader apprehend about the inner reality of the characters and their actions. The readers come to know about the character of the story intensely.

"But he's not my friend! I almost blurted. He's my servant! Had I really thought that? Of course, I hadn't. I hadn't. I treated Hassan well, just like a friend, better even, more like a brother. But if so, then why, when Baba's friends came to visit with their kids, didn't I ever include Hassan in our games? Why did I play with Hassan only when no one else was around?"(Hosseini, p. 38).

These lines depict the real value of Hassan in the life of Amir. When Assef talks about Hassan. He says that Hassan is not his friend but a servant. He plays with Hassan when he uses to be alone. When Amir is with other kids he never allows Hassan to join them. This action shows the deep character of Amir that he is self-centered. The character of Amir is revealed as he can neglect Hassan.

Baba represents the more liberal and to some extent Americanized side of Afghanistan which is against the fundamentalist side whom

Taliban represents. Amir remembers the old days. his friendship with Hassan, the pomegranate tree, the hill, and his carved words, all echoed. Hosseini yearns for peace in Afghanistan. Zahir Shah's time which is lasted for forty years has marked an era of peace and prosperity for Afghanistan.

Semi code implies connotative and figurative meaning to the novel which helps the reader to comprehend the text more easily with its motif. The reoccurring images of kite flying suggest the culture of Afghanistan and merrymaking in Afghanistan.

"At least two dozen kites already hung in the sky, like paper sharks roaming for prey. Within an hour, the number doubled, and red, blue, and yellow kites glided and spun in the sky. A cold breeze wafted through my hair. The wind was perfect for kite flying, blowing just hard enough to give some lift, make the sweeps easier. Next, to me, Hassan held the spool, his hands already bloodied by the string" (Hosseini, p. 60).

These lines show the description of kites and trend of kite flying in Afghanistan as two dozen kites are present in the sky. The kites in different colors are in the sky. A cool breeze lifts them up. Hassan uses to hold the spool. The description of kites shows that kite flying is in the culture of Afghanistan. In their culture marry making, gathering, and kite flying are a crucial part. It is present in their customs.

Semi code aids in understanding the Linguistic structure and figurative language through which the underlying meaning become prominent. The hidden meaning gives essence to the text. The theme of betrayal is understood by Amir's actions.

"Then I took a couple of the envelopes of cash from the pile of gifts and my watch and tiptoed out. I paused before baba's study and listened in. he'd been in there all morning, making phone calls. He was talking to someone now, about a shipment of rugs due to arrive next week. I went downstairs, crossed the yard, and entered Ali and Hassan's mattress and planted my new watch and a handful of Afghani bills under it. I waited another thirty minutes. Then I knocked on Baba's door and told what I hoped would be the last in a long line of shameful lies" (Hosseini, p. 97).

These lines represent the connotative meanings of the actions of Amir. Amir places the envelopes full of money and watches under the mattress of Amir. Amir conspires against Hassan by accusing him in the theft. Amir betrays Hassan because he wants to get rid of from his guilt and Hassan. He plays this game to Hassan for his solace of mind and soul. He wants his burden shed off which he feeling by watching Hassan.

The semantic code deals with the description of farfetched ideas, monsters, vampires, exaggerations, and imaginative things. In the novel, Amir dreams about the monster and considers him that monster. "There is no monster, he'd said, just water, except he'd been wrong about that. There was a monster in the lake. It had grabbed Hassan by the ankles, dragged him to the murky bottom. I was that monster" (Hosseini, p. 80-81). In these lines, Amir thinks about the monster which he sees in his dream. The monster grabs the ankles of Hassan and drags him. The description of the monster and an abnormal creature is techniques which maintain the interest of readers in the story.

Assef symbolized as the negative force in the text. He is the sign of terror and violence in the story. He dislikes even hates Hazaras. He is violent and bullying. He is racist and prejudiced against Hassan.

Amir is jealous of Hasan who is a favorite of Baba. Amir is desperate for Baba's approval. Kite fighting tournament is a great opportunity to win the favors of Baba. The blue kite gains some special status. Amir has to defeat that blue kite to restore his image. Ultimately Amir wins and he now sure to win Baba's love when Hassan brings back the losing kite. " snow crunching under his black rubber boots. He was yelling over his shoulder: For you, thousand times over!" (Hosseini,2013,p.194). Hassan parting words have special meaning as it shows his selflessness and unconditional love and devotion to Amir. Rostam and Sohrab represent the archetypal relationship of father and son in the east. It also sheds light on the relations of Amir and Baba. Amir's reluctance and inability to safe Hassan have multilayered meanings. It also suggests his inner desire to give and suffering to Hassan. He also wants in his subconscious, revenge over Hassan for having a better position in the eyes of Baba. Assef's remarks about Amir shows Amir's darker side.

The rape of Hassan has other meaning also. It also suggests the rape of Afghanistan by his own extremists and fundamentalists. It also signifies the suffering of Hazaras by the hands of Pashtuns. It also suggests coming violence and bloodshed to Afghanistan, when the weak will be raped by the powerful extremists. Hassan is a sacrificial lamb, like Jesus. He is the victim of abused power in the text. Amir sacrifices his best friend for the blue kite to win Baba's favor. It also suggests the end of the ere of innocence and childhood in Afghanistan.

Amir tries to move Hassan to punish him in the hope that it might make him feel good and normal. But Hassan's love and loyalty are unwavering. It makes Amir weak and cowardly compared with Hassan. When the power shift occurred, people like Assef got control to act any cruel whim. Now he was able to perform a larger rape to Afghanistan. Baba hates confusion and lawlessness. He always prefers death over lack of principles in life. He even confronts Russian soldier. He is a true patriot. he kisses the soil of

Afghanistan. He mourns for the country which is destroying itself. In America also Baba is disgusted at the lack of high moral standards in the society.

Baba feels loneliness, uprootedness, and disconnection in California. But for Amir, this disconnection is healthy as it helps him to forget his guilty past. Now he can focus on his dream of becoming a writer. America is described as a river, where he is baptized from his past sins. He is washing away dirt and sins from his soul. He is trying to reborn himself by pursuing writing as a career. Here an important character enters into the life of the protagonist, Soraya. Hosseini uses her to comment on the Afghan society's double standards regarding genders. Involvement of women with a man outside the marriage is taken something of shame and gossip is followed by but men are allowed to do anything in any way.

Amir starts falling in love with Soraya. By this episode of working Hosseini painted the Afghan culture, which is still maintaining their traditions even in America.

Baba's fight with cancer and ultimate acceptance of defeat and death but in an honorable way gives grace and charm to the text. Soraya past relation is a horrible scandal for an Afghan woman. According to Afghan standards, she has lost the true value of an honorable woman. Amir accepts Soraya and defies Afghan false standards regarding honor and woman. His own past sins make him able to accept other persons past mistakes. Here at that happy moments interrupted by a phone call from Pakistan and subsequent narrative shifts.

Two things are making Amir sick, his past and his inability to have a child with Soraya. He feels an emptiness in his life. Amir shocks when returning to Afghanistan, to see the rubble state of his country. Amir is informed about Hassan, his marriage with Farzana, bearing a child and their horrible death by the hands of the Taliban. There is extreme lawlessness as there was no punishment for those who murdered Hassan and Farzana.

This time Amir does not escape from the troubles but faces them boldly. By protecting Sohrab he can redeem himself from his past cowardice. Assef again abusing and raping Hassan in the form of

Sohrab. The whole terrible past is returned in the shape of Assef. Assef joins the Taliban because they give him free hand to practice violence. Amir shows the coward self of Afghanistan and Assef signifies the violent self of Afghanistan. But now Amir is stood up to stop the violence in the society. The beating of Amir retrieved his lost self. Now he has become a man who is wrestling with a dangerous violent bear. He is now able to face the terror and handle the atrocities. In a way, he is a Pashtun who is fighting for a Hazara.

Sohrab is broken inside. He is unable to cope with life due to frequent rapes. Amir builds a father-son relationship with Sohrab to break the cycle of betrayal and lies. Sohrab's try to commit suicide shocks, Amir. Amir needs religion he has always struggled with. He accepts God who forgives and heals. Amir decides to help and work for his homeland, Afghanistan. Kites at the end of the narrative represent hope for the better future for Afghanistan.

The semantic code uses the technique of conceit to convey underlying meanings. As in, the novel some countries are called men and some are called women. "There are only three real men in this world, Amir", he'd say. He'd count them off on his fingers: America the brash savior, Britain, and, Israel. "The rest of them – he used to wave his hand and make a *phht* sound" they're like gossiping old women"(Hosseini, p. 116). In these lines, Agha Jan considers America, Britain, and Israel as real men and brave. While on the other hand, he considers other countries as women. For him other countries just make gossips but only three countries work like men. These personifications are used in the novel to give proper meaning without boredom.

4.4.2.Conclusion

This chapter studies the Semantic code in Hosseini's masterpiece, *The Kite Runner*. The present chapter analyzes the text through the voice of a person. The semantic code also called the "voice of a person". It deals with exaggerated elements in the text. The code argues that elements which create strangeness formulate the plot of the novel.

4.5. Exploration of Cultural code (REF)

The present chapter aims to study the cultural code given by Roland Barthes and applied to the text of *The Kite Runner* written by Khalid Hosseini. This chapter studies the novel through this particular perspective to explore the references of sciences, arts, history, tradition, and literature. The researcher applies the Cultural code which is also called Referential code. Barthes in his book *S/Z* suggests that Cultural code helps the reader to know about the psychology, culture, medical, literary and historical knowledge. This chapter finds out the tradition of marrying making, songs, poetry, weddings, kite flying, and Eid Celebration. These cultures and traditions show the zeal of Afghanis to keep their tradition alive.

4.5.1. Data Analysis

Cultural code plays an important role in the narrative. It is also known as Referential code. It refers to the elements which help to share knowledge. "By this code, a reader gets the physical, physiological, medical, psychological, literary or historical knowledge. The gnomic code is one of the cultural codes and refers to those cultural codes that are tied to clichés, proverbs or popular sayings of various sorts" (Felluga, n.d.). It helps to classify the common knowledge shared in the text.

In the very first chapter the protagonist, Amir provides a framework for the rest of the text. Amir, who has been living in American for two decades just receives a phone call from Rahim Khan. He is forced to come back and face the mess. He can listen to the whisper of Hassan in his ear, " For you, a thousand times over"(Hosseni, 2013, p. 67). It shows something had happened on a frosty overcast day, in the winter of 1975. Those incidents play an important part of what he is now.

In the novel *The Kite Runner* by Khalid Hosseini, the reader comes to know about Muslim culture through the description of Mullah Fatiullah Khan and his teachings of Islam.

"When I was in fifth grade, we had a mullah who taught us about Islam. His name was Mullah Fatiullah Khan, a short stubby man with a face full of acne scars and gruff voice. He lectured us about the virtues of *zakat* and duty of hadj; he taught us the intricacies of performing the five daily *namaz* prayers and made us memorize verses from the Koran"(Hosseini, p. 15).

These lines suggest that the reader comes to know about the culture of Muslims through the description of Mullah Sahib's teachings of Islam. Amir says that Mullah teaches them about Islam, Hajj, Zakat, and Namaz. He also teaches them about the verses of the Quran. This shows that it is a culture of Muslims to know about the basic pillars of Islam and to memorize the verses of Quran. It is a tradition in Islamic society that a Mullah is hired to teach the Quran. In Muslim culture, it is necessary to learn about Islam and the Quran.

Through cultural code reader also comes to know about the literary knowledge of the particular society. In the novel, Amir talks about the game which is called a battle of poems. Through reference to the poets, the reader knows about the literary knowledge. Literary knowledge shows the culture of a society. "I could recite dozen of verses from Khayyam, Hafez, or Rumi's famous Masnavi" (Hosseini, p.18). The references of poets show the culture of Afghan that people are found of poems and poets. The references of Hafez, Rumi, and Khayyam show a keen interest in Muslim poet and the tradition of reading poetry in Afghanistan.

The cultural code of Barthes helps the reader to know about the trends and psychology of people. In the novel, the celebration of Eid and greetings show the culture of Muslims in Afghanistan. " On Eid, the three days of celebration after the holy month of Ramadan, Kabulis dressed in their best and newest clothes greeted each other with "Eid Mubarak". Happy Eid. Children opened gifts and played with dyed hard-boiled eggs" (Hosseini, p. 41). These lines depict the culture of celebrating the holy day of Eid after the holy month of Ramadan. Kabuli dresses are worn by people. People greet each other with passion and zeal. Children receive their gifts and play. The celebration of Eid indicates the importance of making joy. It shows the Muslim culture's effort to bring people together.

This code reveals about the culture of a society. Kite flying is a dominant culture in the society of Afghanistan. Kite flying is a symbol of marrying making. It indicates marry making is a tradition of Afghan culture.

"At least two dozen kites already hung in the sky, like paper sharks roaming for prey. Within an hour, the number doubled, and red and yellow kites glided and spun in the sky. A cold breeze through my hair. The wind was perfect for kite flying, blowing just hard enough to give some lift, make the sweeps easier" (Hosseini, p. 59-60).

Above mentioned lines show the tradition of festivals and merrymaking in the society of Afghanistan. The narrator describes dozens of kites float on the sky. These kites seem that they are searching for a victim. Some kites are red some are blue and some kites are yellow. The wind is also in favor of kites. The culture and tradition of marrying making show that the people of Afghanistan enjoy the festivals.

Ali is a Hazara and also belongs to Shi's Muslim. He is also physically deformed. They have to endure discrimination because they belong to the minority in the Kabul. Here Hosseini exposes the social structure of the society at that time. ethnicity and racism was part of the daily life of Kabul.

Through cultural code, the reader knows about the psychology of society. In the novel, the reader comes to know about the psychology of the people of Afghanistan. Afghanis prefer to sit together and share their things. The reason behind the tradition is to create love among the people. "The wives and daughters served dinner- rice, kofta and chicken qurma- at sundown. We dined the traditional way, sitting on cushions around the room, tablecloth spread on the floor, eating with our hands in groups of four or five from common platters" (Hosseini, 2013, p. 80). In these lines the tradition of sitting together and to have food designate the sharing nature of people. The sophisticated nature and well-mannered behavior show the mindset of people. They bring people closer to each other. They eat in the same plate to increase the love among themselves.

Baba is a rich person in the Kabul, who owns different types of businesses, e.g a restaurant, a carpet exporting business, and an orphanage. Baba, himself is a physically strong and psychologically brave person but he always feels concerns about his son, Amir. Hosseini shows that Afghanistan is the land of tough people. Here only brace, strong and hard persons can stand against the difficult environment of the land. That is why he does not like his son to become a writer. Baba never mentioned Ali as his friend and Amir also hesitate to accept Hassan as his brother. This shows their consciousness about ethnic superiority.

Amir's favorite story is Rustom and Sohrab. It refers to the traditional story of father and son. It also sheds light on the relationship between Amir and his father. It is also significant that later in the text, Hassan names his son, Sohrab. Eastern fathers inherent desire to sacrifice his own son is also discussed in the background of Rustom and Sohrab.

In the novel, the song is also mentioned to help the reader to know about the importance of joy and inclination to pleasure in the lives of people in Afghanistan. The song is itself a product of a culture and shows the approach of the people of the society.

The laughing man broke into song, a slurring, off-key rendition of an old Afghan wedding song delivered with a thick Russian accent:

Ahesta boro, mah-e-man, Chester Boro

Go slowly, my lovely moon, go slowly (Hosseini, p. 105-106).

These lines elucidate the tradition of songs in Afghanistan. The quality of marrying making, joy, and happiness is present in the blood of Pashtuns. The song tells us about the approach of people that they find some solution of joy in a troublesome moment.

The referential code indicates that the people of Afghanistan have a tradition of songs and festivals. At the wedding of Suraya and Amir the song is sung. The song is part of their culture which shows the efficiency of Afghans in literature.

"The wedding song Shasta boro, blared from the speakers, the same song the Russian soldier at the Mahipar checkpoint had sung the night baba and I left Kabul:

Make morning into a key and throw it into the well,

Go slowly, my lovely moon, go slowly.

Let the morning sun forget to rise in the east,

Go slowly, my lovely moon, go slowly" (Hosseini, p. 157).

These lines elucidate that the weddings of Afghanis and Muslims are not simple. Muslim weddings also possess songs and poetry. As the cousin of Soraya sings the same song that Russian Soldier sang. The joyful song shows that Afghans enjoy their weddings and celebrate the events through the help of literature.

Amir and Hassan's conversation is disrupted by the violent sounds of gunfires. There is a bloodless coup, in which Daud Khan, overthrows his cousin King Zahir, to establish a Rebuplic. But only eighteen months later Russians invades Afghanistan. The political history is painted in the background of the personal lives of characters.

Assef brags about the new leader of the country and he says that his favorite leader is Hitler. He hates Hazaras and shows openly is disgust and plans to clean Afghanistan from Hazara people. He threatens Hassan many times and even worse once raped the boy.

Baba arranges a plastic Surgeon to repair his cleft lif, from Indian in the winter of 1974 at Hassan's birthday. In winter schools are closed and people are interested in Kite flying tournament. It is a cultural event. All the sky of Kabul in winter seems full of colors of kites. Baba wishes, Amir to win the biggest tournament of kite fighting. In order to cut the opponents kites, the strings are coated with glue and glass. Hassan is the greatest kite runner ever. He has many kites in his possession. He knows intuitively where the kite will land after the cut. In the frosty winter of 1975, Hassan runs for a kite, for the last time.

Amir looks for his kite and Hassan and finds him in an alley walled by Assef and his group. Assef then sodomizes Hassan. This incident changes the course of the narrative and the lives of the main character, Amir and Hassan. Later Baba throws a lavish party at the birthday of Amir where Amir receives gifts, a biography of Hiter from Assef, a notebook from Rahim Khan and Shahnama, from Hassan.

By March of 1981 the political condition of the country declines to that point where "You couldn't trust anyone in Kabul anymore—for a fee or under threat, people told on each other, neighbor on neighbor, child on parent, brother on brother, servant on master, friend on friend" (Hosseini ,2013,p.112). Baba now makes arrangements to leave Afghanistan. Hosseini sheds light on the condition of the war-torn country and its people who flee from the country to other safe areas, and how they suffer and face pains in their lives.

Baba said. He said it to Karim but looked directly at the Russian officer. "Ask him where his shame is." They spoke. "He says this is war. There is no shame in war." "Tell him he's wrong. War doesn't negate decency. It demands it, even more than in times of peace"(Hosseini, 2013, p.115).

The refugees are bound to hide in dungeon basements or travel in fuel tanks, without proper food and water. Hosseini narrates that many people died, many women are raped and many children are kidnapped. Hosseini painted a horrific picture of war and bloodshed in Afghanistan. Baba migrated to America with Amir. But Amir says, "For me, America was a place to bury my memories. For Baba, a place to mourn his" (Hosseini 2013,p.129). this statement expresses the trauma facing by the diaspora, living in America.

Amir encounters the beautiful and charming Soraya, at the flea market. He instantly infatuated by her charming beauty. Every coming night turns to a Yelda for him. It is a traditional reference which means "Yelda was the starless night tormented lovers kept vigil, enduring the endless dark, waiting for the sun to rise and bring with it their loved one" (Hosseini, 2013, p. 143). The event of marriage has been arranged by Baba, who understands the heart of Amir about Soraya. But before marriage Soraya exposes her dark side of the past, the elopement of her with a man and living with him for a month. But Amir realizes that "there were many ways in which Soraya Taheri was a better person than me. Courage was just one of them" (Hosseini, 2013, p.165). The Lafz or the ceremony of giving words show the Afghan tradition of getting married. Their concept of honor and prestige. Their dresses, talks, celebrations, are Afghan in nature though they are in America now. Although shirini khri or eating of the sweets, dance, and songs are curtailed due to the sickness of Baba. For the awroussi or the wedding ceremony, Baba spent 35000 dollars, all his savings.

After Baba's death, Amir focuses on writing and in 1088 he published in the first story which make him a small celebrity in the Afghan community. Amir decides to visit Pakistan, after the call of Rahim Khan, and from there he visits Afghanistan. And discovered the horrible condition of his beloved country. War, the Russian invasion, the Taliban's brutality in Afghanistan turned the country in a ruins state. To his dismay, they also killed Hassan and his wife Farzana. Baba's Orphanage is also destroyed by war. Taliban's brutality and their lack of sense of history are demonstrated when it is mentioned that they destroyed the Budha largest statue in Bamiyan. "What heritage?" I said. "The Taliban have destroyed what heritage Afghans had. You saw what they did to the giant Buddhas in Bamiyan"(Hosseini 2013, p.337). They damaged the spiritual and rich cultural history of the country.

Taliban also banned kite fighting in Kabul. But ironically they allowed ethnic cleansing and massacred of the Hazaras in Mazar I Sharif. The slice of history is presented by the author in the text of the novel.

Amir is terrified to see the country in the state of rubbles and devastations all around, by Russians and Taliban. Amir is shocked to see "the beggars were mostly children now, thin and grim-faced, some no older than five or six. They sat in the laps of their burqa-clad mothers alongside gutters at busy street corners and chanted Bakhshesh, bakhshish!" (Hosseini, 2013,p. 245). The playground and football stadiums are converted to kill innocent persons. Amir can see corpse at every corner of the country. Amir meets Assef, who is turned now a Taliban general. Taliban give free hand to do any violent practice to Assef. Assef beats Amir badly, breaks his nose and teeth but Amir starts laughing. Finally, Amir sheds his cowardice and faces the danger eye in the eye. He feels relieved from his past coward actions. His laughing angers Assef more. The fight ends when Sohrab slingshot at Assef, and takes out his eye.

Last closing scene is about the kite flying, when in March 2002, at a party arranged by the American Afghan community, Amir buys a kite for Sohrab. Two of them win the kite fighting contest, just as he and Hassan had done many years ago in Kabul.

Now Amir runs the kite for Sohrab and Sohrab smiles for the first time for Amir.

4.5.2. Conclusion

The chapter studies the Cultural code of Barthes in Hosseini's masterpiece. The present chapter investigates the text through the lens of Cultural code. The Cultural code helps the reader to know about the tradition of a particular society. The study finds out that the culture of Afghanistan is joyful and brings people together.

Chapter 05

Conclusion/Findings

The researcher took the text of the novel, *The Kite Runner* to explored the structure of the narrative. It is the exposure of the structuration of the structures inherent in the text of *The Kite Runner*. The theory of five codes proposed by Roland Barthes has been used by the researcher. Five codes are in analogy with the five senses of human beings, which enable them to understand the world around. Together, these five codes function as a "weaving of voices," as Barthes puts it (ibid.p. 20). Following five codes have been used for detailed analysis: Proairetic code, Hermeneutic code, Symbolic code, Semantic code, and Cultural code. The main objective was to explore the narrative structure of the text. As

Barthes states that "The voices or codes point to the "multivalence of the text" and to "its partial reversibility" (ibid. p.20). no fixed meanings are found. Structurally it is closed to the readerly text. But text contains polyphonic quality. To Barthes," trying to assign a specific origin to text is impossible, as literary works always display multiple voices. Therefore, he argued that one definite interpretation is impossible" (Barthes,p. 2).

The researcher finds that all five codes are working within the selected text. The study was qualitative in nature. The selected text is analyzed under the light of all codes, one by one. Khaled Hosseini designed a balanced artwork in the form of *The Kite Runner*. The researcher formed his own method to apply the five codes to the selected text. the researcher divides the analysis into five subparts based on five codes. It is exploratory researcher the narrative of the novel has been analyzed from five dimensions.

Khaled Hosseini's The Kite Runner has never been explored structurally. So there was a researcher gap and the present study is an effort to fill that gap. It is a significant effort which proves that The narrative is not a random assemblage of events rather it has a structure. It is a common structure to all narrative. it is code working behind all the narratives. This researcher proves and confirms the theory or thesis of Roland Barthes.

The present study discusses the narrative structure of *The Kite Runner* by Khaled Hosseini. It discovers the binary oppositions playing a pivotal role in the constructing meanings of the text. it hits the cognitive linguistics from that side. How the human mind works to understand the meanings of a narrative. This study points out the elements in the narrative which has the quality of gripping the mind of the reader to read further till the end. It discusses the role of Hermeneutic code to catch the mind of the reader. It also discusses the plot of the novel how it is constructed, how it moves further and develops. It is also explored the meaning created by the authors and the contribution of the author, the awesome and supernatural, or abnormal elements in the text of the novel which are purely added by the author's imagination. It is also discussed that cultural, historical, political, scientific, and literary texts also play a very important part in the construction of the next.

The most important objective of the thesis was to explore the Five Codes (Proairetic, Hermeneutic, Semantic, Symbolic, and Cultural Code) working behind the apparent story of the novel, *The Kite Runner*. The researcher applied five codes and found that the relations of meaning, binary and human cognition. The readers understand the text in the light of binaries within the text. as good is recognized in the opposition of the evil. And it is discovered that the voice of the culture is playing an important role in the construction of the text of the novel. The kite flying and then running is a cultural event in Afghan society. They love poetry, music, and Dastan's. The researcher also traced the Seme given by the author.

In the present thesis, the researcher carefully works to disassemble a popular novel, *The Kite Runner* by Khaled Hosseini. The researcher found that the text of *The Kite Runner* has plural quality. Its signifiers can be grouped into five subparts. The key elements of the text show decentralization and plurality having five voices in the text. Meaning are produced by binary opposition within the structure of the text. Every reader can associate and understand different meaning according to his her own cultural understand and knowledge. Apparently, the text seems to have stable meaning but the researcher after deep analysis of the structure finds various voices interwoven in the text. "this ideal text is a galaxy of signifiers, not a structure of signifieds" (*S/Z* 1970, p.5). the text of the narrative does not hold an ultimate signified. It does not offer a central meaning. The narrative has formed a surface on the concept of linearity solidarity and the principle of non-contradiction. But deep structure shows its lack of central meaning and solidness. There is a semantic cohesion. The intersections of various codes under the surfaces exposes its polyphonic quality. The researcher explored, plural quality, multiplicity, and decentralization. The text of The Kite Runner is polyphonic.

Five codes are explored. Three of them (semic, symbolic and cultural code) established reversible connections, outside the constraint of time. And the other two (hermeneutic and proairetic code) imposed terms in an irreversible order *the kite runner* is a classic text because it like all classic text it follows a logical temporal order.

The researcher finds that *The Kite Runner* is an artistic work. It does not propagate, politics, history, philosophy or ethnic discourse. "...the meaning of a text lies not in this or that interpretation but in the diagrammatic totality of its readings, in their plural system" (Barthes, p. 120). *The Kite Runner* is not a book of history, philosophy or politics. It is a novel. It is a fiction. The main purpose of fiction is to produce art. Art means the creation of beauty. The main purpose of beauty is to give pleasure, to spread happiness and joy. Sublime art gives eternal pleasure and joy to the readers or viewers. As John Keats says

"A thing of beauty is a joy forever:

Its loveliness increases; it will never

Pass into nothingness;"

(*The Poetical works of Johan Keats*, Endymion, Book I, p.66).

REFERENCES

Arani, F. S. *The Play of Codes and Systems in Pygmalion: Bernard Shaw and Roland Barthes.* Iran: Institute of Higher Education Isfahan.

Asghar, M. M. (2014). *The Role of Linguistic Devices in Representing Ethnicity in The Kite Runner.*

Abrams, M. H. (1990). *A Glossary of Literary Terms.* London: Thomas Heinle.

Ahmad, W. (2018). *Thematic study of Khalid Hosseini's novel The Kite Runner.*

Ahmadi, B. (2015). *The Text- Structure and Text Interpretation.* Tehran. Markaz.

Alighieri, D. (1996). *The Divine Comedy* (Robert M. Durling, Trans.). New York, NY: Oxford   University Press.

Allen, G. (2003). *Roland Barthes.* New York: Routledge.

Arani, F. S. *The Play of Codes and Systems in Pygmalion: Bernard Shaw and Roland Barthes.* Iran: Institute of Higher Education Isfahan.

Asghar, M. M. (2014). *The Role of Linguistic Devices in Representing Ethnicity in The Kite Runner.*

Atashsoda, Mohammad Ali. (2012). *Semiotic Analysis of 'Sheikh San'an'. Journal of* *Boostan-e-Adab*: pp. 11-22.

Attar, Farid ud-Din. (1984). *The Conference of The Birds.* Trans. Afghan Darbandi and Dick Davis. London: Penguin.

Bagheri Khalili, A. & Zabihpor, S. (2015). Structural Analysis a sign in contrast to the lyrics of Hafez relied on the theory of Roland Barthes. Journal of Persian Language and Literature No 35. Barthes, Ronald([1973]1974): S/Z London; Cape.

Booryazadeh, S. A. (2013). Barthes Irreversible codes: An Intertextual Reading of James Joyce.   Iran: Vali-e-Asr University.

Barthes, Roland. 1972. *Critical Essays*.   Evanston, Illinois: Northwestern University Press.

Barthes, Roland. 1973. *Elements of Semiology*. New York: Hill and Wang.

Barthes, Roland. 1977. *Image-Music-Text*. Washington: Fontana Press.

Barthes, R. (1977). *Image-Music-Text*. London: Fontana.

Barry, P. (2002). *Beginning Theory: An Introduction to Literary and Cultural Theory* (2nd Ed).

    Manchester: Manchester UP.

Barthes, R. *S/Z*. Miller, R. (1974). (Trans.) New York: Hill and

Wang.

Barthes, R. & Duisit, L. (1975). *An Introduction to the Structural Analysis of Narrative,*

New Literary History, 6(2): 237-272.

Barthes, R. (1977). *The Death of the Author. In Image, Music Text.* Heath, S. (Trans.). London:

Fontana Press.

Birch, D. (1989). Language, Literature and Critical Practice. London & NY: Routledge.

Baldick, C. (2004). *The Concise Oxford Dictionary of literary terms,* viewed 8 March 2011, http://www.highbeam.com/doc/1056-binaryopposition.html

Barry, P. (2002). *Beginning theory: An introduction to the literary and cultural theory.* 2nded. Manchester: Manchester UP.

Barthes, R. (1972). *Critical Essays.* Evanston, Illinois: Northwestern University Press.

Barthes, R. (1972). Mythologies. Trans. Annette Lavers. New York: Hill and Wang: 119.

Barthes, R. (1973). _Elements of Semiology_. New York: Hill and Wang.

Barthes, R. (1974). _S/Z_. New York: Blackwell.

Barthes, R. (1973-1974): S/Z London; Cape.

Barthes, R. (1974). S/Z. (R., Miller, Trans). London: Blackwell Publishing Ltd.

Barthes, R. & Duisit, L. (1975). An Introduction to the Structural Analysis of Narrative, New Literary History, 6(2): pp. 237-272.

Barthes, R. (1976). S/Z Trans. Jurgen Hoch. Suhrkamp

Barthes, R. (1977). Image–Music–Text. London: Fontana Press.

Barthes, R. (1977). _The Death of the Author. In Image, Music Text._ Heath, S. (Trans.). London: Fontana Press.

Barthes, R. (1977). _Inaugural Lecture._ Collège de France.

Barthes, R. (1977). _Roland Barthes._ Trans. Richard Howard.

London: Macmillan,177.

Barthes, R. (1990). *S/Z*. United Kingdom: Blackwell Publishers.

Barthes, R. (1990*)*. *S/Z* (Richard Miller, Trans.). Oxford: Blackwell.

Barthes, R. (2013). *Mythologies*. Translated Dakhikhiyan, Shirin. Tehran. Markaz.

Barthes, R. (1971). *From Work to Text*. The Rustle of Language. Translated Richard Howard. New York: Hill & Wang, 1986. 56-64.

Belsey, C. (2002). *Post-structuralism: A very short introduction*. New York, Oxford.U P.

Benoist, Jean-Marie. (1978). *The Structural Revolution.Trans*. A.Pomeranz.London: Weidenfeld and Nicolson.

Blackburn, S. (2008). *Oxford Dictionary of Philosophy*, second edition revised. Oxford: Oxford University Press, ISBN 978-0-19-954143-0.

Booryazadeh, S. A. (2013). *Barthes Irreversible codes: An Intertextual Reading of James Joyes*. Iran: Vali-e-Asr University.

Boysen, B. (2008). *The Necropolis of Love: James Joyce's Dubliners.* Neohelicon 36 (1), 157-169.

Bozorg-e-Bigdeli, Saeed & Ehsan Pourabrisham. (2011*). Analysis of 'Sheikh San'an'*

in Terms of Carl Jung Individuation Process. Mythology and Mystic Literature: pp. 9-38.

Bulson, E. (2006). The Cambridge Introduction to James Joyce. New York, NY: Cambridge University Press.

Burke, S. (1998). *The Death and Return of the Author*: Criticism and Subjectivity in Barthes, Foucault, and Derrida. Edinburgh: Edinburgh University Press.

Buswell. G. (2015). *An introduction to Jude the Obscure.* Retrieved from http://www.bl.uk/romantics-and-victorians/articles/an-introduction-to-jude-theobscure April 4, 2016.

Campbell, Joseph. (1949). The *Hero with a Thousand Faces*. Princeton: Princeton University Press, 1972.

Chabha, A. A. (2014). *Death of the Author and Birth of the Reader in Thomas Hardy's Jude the Obscure*. Ouargle: KasdiMerbah University.

Chabha, A. A. (2014). *Death of the Author and Birth of the Reader in Thomas Hardy's Jude the Obscure*. Ouargle: KasdiMerbah University.

Champagne, Roland A. *Between Orpheus and Eurydice*: Roland Barthes and the Historicity of Reading. Clio, 8.2. 1979.

Chandler, D. (2007). *Semiotics: The Basics*. (2nd ed.). New York, NY: Routledge.

Charles, E. Bressler. (2004). *Literary Criticism: An Introduction to the Theory and Practice* [M]. Beijing: Higher Education Press. Retrieved from https://en.m.wikipedia.org/wiki/Structuralism.

Collins, B. L. (1968). *"Araby" and the Extended Similie*. In Peter K. Garrett (Ed.), Twentieth Century Interpretations of Dubliners

(93-99) Englewood Cliffs: Prentice-Hall, Inc.

Culler, J. (1975). *Structuralist Poetics: Structuralism, Linguistics and the study of Literature.* London and New York, NY: Routledge.

Davidson, G. W. & Seaton, M. A. (Eds). (n.d.). *Chambers pocket 20th-century dictionary.* Edinburgh: W & R Chambers Ltd.

Davor Džalto. (2015). *Art: A brief history of absence.* From the Conception and Birth, Life and Death, to the Living Deadness of Art.

Dawkins, Richard. (1976). *The Selfish Gene. Oxford:* Oxford University Press.

Deleuze, G. (2002). *How Do We Recognise Structuralism?* In the Desert Islands and Other Texts 1953-1974. Trans.

de Man, Paul. 1971. *Blindness and Insight: Essays in Rhetoric of Contemporary Criticism*, New York: Oxford University Press.

de Man, Paul. 1986. *The Resistance to Theory.* London: University of Minnesota Press.

Derrida, Jacques. 1976. *Of Grammatology*. Baltimore & London: Johns Hopkins University Press.

De Man, Paul. (1971). *Blindness and Insight: Essays in Rhetoric of Contemporary Criticism*, New York: Oxford University Press.

De Man, Paul. (1986). *The Resistance to Theory*. London: University of Minnesota Press.

Derrida, Jacques. (1976). *Of Grammatology*. Baltimore & London: Johns Hopkins University Press.

Doland, Angela. (2009). Anthropology giant Claude Levi Strauss dead at 100. Seattle Times. Associated Press. Retrieved 22 April 2015.

Doloff, S. (1995). Aspects of Milton's Paradise Lost in James Joyce's "Araby." James Joyce Quarterly, 33 (1), 113-115.

Duncan, Randy. *Shape and Color as Hermeneutic Images in Asterios Polyp*. In Critical
Approaches to Comics: Theories and Methods, edited by Matthew J. Smith and Randy Duncan. New York: Routledge, 2012.

Eagleton, T. (1996). *Literary Theory: An Introduction (2nd ed.)* Minnesota: University of Minnesota.

Eagleton, T. (1996). *Literary Theory: An Introduction (2nd ed.)* Minnesota: University of Minnesota.

Ellis, John. *The Literary Adaptation*: An Introduction. Screen 23.1, 1982: 4-5.

Farina, N. (2008). *The issue of cultural identity in Khaled Hosseini's The Kite Runner.* Jakarta: University Syarif Hidayatullah Jakarta.

Fish, S. (1970). *Literature in the Reader:* Affective Stylistics. Tompkins, Reader-Response Criticism.

Fogarty, S. (2005).*The literary encyclopedia.* Retrieved from http://www.litencyc.com/php/stopics.php? pec = true & UID=122 6 March 2011.

Foucault, Michel. *"What Is an Author?" Language, Counter-memory, Practice.* Ed. Donald F. Bouchard, Trans. D. F. Bouchard, Sherry Simon. New York: Cornell University Press,

1977. 113-38.

F.Soltani. (2014). *An Analysis of Sheikh Sanaan's Story Based on Roland Barthes's Theory of codes.* Iran: Sobh-e-Sadegh Institute of Higher Education Isfahan.

Farina, N. (2008). *The issue of cultural identity in Khaled Hosseini's The Kite Runner.* Jakarta: University Syarif Hidayatullah Jakarta.

Frasca, Gonzalo. Simulation versus narrative. The video game theory reader (2003): 227.

Gagnier. R. (1991). (as cited in Wolfreys' *Critical Keywords in Literary and Cultural Theory,*

2004).

Goldstein. P. (2005). *Reader-Response Theory: Death of The Author and Criticism.* The Johns Hopkins University Press. Ed. 2nd.

Gallop. J. (2011). *The Deaths of the Author: Reading and Writing in Time.* Durham & London: Duke University Press.

Genette, Girard. (1997). *Paratexts. Translated Jane E. Lewin.* Cambridge: Cambridge University Press

Ghahreman, O. (2013). *James Joyce's "An Encounter": From the Perversion of an Escape to the Perversion of the Fatherhood.* International Journal of Applied Linguistics & English Literature, 2 (2), 158-164.

Gholizadeh, Heidar. (2008). Reconstruction of 'Sheikh San'an'. *Kavooshnameh*: pp.129-162.

Graf, Fritz. (2002). *Myth in Ovid.* In The Cambridge Companion to Ovid, ed. Philip Hardie. Cambridge: Cambridge University Press. Pp. 108-121.

Harris, Wendell. (1992). *Structuralism."Dictionary of Concepts in Literary Criticism and Theory.*New York: Greenwood Press. Pp. 378-387.

Hashemi, Mansour. 2004. *The Theory of Epistemological Transmutation of English Language.* Unpublished doctoral dissertation, The University of Birmingham.

HenrikssonÅsa". *The rEADER sTRIKES bACK A Narratological Approach to Paul Auster's The NewYork Theology.* Goteborg Universities.

Hashemi, Mansour. (2004). *The Theory of Epistemological Transmutation of English Language.* Unpublished doctoral dissertation, The University of Birmingham.

Haskins, S. (1995). *Mary Magdalene Myth and Metaphor.* New York, NY: The Berkley Publishing Group.

Heath, Stephen. (1971). *A conversation with Roland Barthes. Signs of the Times: Introductory Readings in Textual Semiotics.* ed. Heath, Stephen, Colin MacCabe, and Christopher Prendergast.

Herring, P. F. (1987). *Joyce's Uncertainty Principle.* Princeton: Princeton University Press.

Holland, Michael. (1988). *Barthes, Orpheus...* Paragraph 11.2. pp. 143-74.

Holland. N. (1975). Reading and Identity. Retrieved from

http://users.clas.ufl.edu/nholland/rdgident.htm. 12 03, 2016.

Hussein, J. (2009). The Nation Newspaper Retrieved from http//:nation.com.pk/Lahore/09november2009/Taufiq-Rafat-the-Ezra-Pond-of–Pakistan April 20, 2016.

Hutcheon, Linda. (2006). *A Theory of Adaptation.* New York: Routledge.

Jabarbahman, M. (2017). *Image of Islam in postcolonial Novel: E.M> Forster's A Passage to India and Khaled Hosseini's The Kite Runner Journal of Raparin University.* Raparin University.

Jamshidian, Homayoon & Leila Noroozpour. (2012). Examination of Representation of Meaning in the Surface of 'Sheikh San'an'. *Bahar-e-Adab*: pp.109-128.

Jean, Piaget. (1968). Le structuralism, ed. PDF.

Jenkins, D. (2003). The Cambridge History of Western Textile, New York: Cambridge University Press.

Jabarbahman, M. (2017). *Image of Islam in postcolonial Novel: E.M> Forster's A passage to India and Khaled Hosseini's The Kite Runner Journal of Raparin University*. Raparin Universty.

Johnson, Barbara. (1978). *The Critical Difference*. Diacritics, 8.2. pp. 2-9.

Joyce, J. (2005). Dubliners, Webster's Thesaurus (Ed.). San Diego: ICON Group International, Inc.

Joyce, J. (1944). *Stephan Hero*. London: Jonathan Cape Limited.

Juul, Jesper. (2001). *Games Telling Stories*. Game Studies 1.1.

Khaled, H. (2004). *The Kite Runner*. Bloomsbury Publishing.

Khoirun, F. z. (2014). *Child Abuse in Khalid Hosseini's The Kite runner*. Malanga: Maulana Malik Ibrahim Islamic state University

.

Khoirun, F. z. (2014). *Child Abuse in Khalid Hosseini's The Kite runner*. Malanga: Maulana Malik Ibrahim Islamic State University.

Lacan, Jacques, et al. (2006*). Écrits: The first complete edition in English*. New York: WW Norton & Co.

Lacey, N. (2000). *Narrative and Genre,* p.64, Palgrave, New York.

Smith, G. *(1996). Binary opposition and sexual power in Paradise Lost. Midwest Quarterly. 27 (4): 383*

Lambert, Deborah G. (1986*). S/Z: Barthes' Castration Camp and the Discourse of Polarity.*
Modern Language Studies: 161-171.

Lashari, M. A., Afsar, A. & Sangi, M. K. (2012). Theory into Practice: Narrative Analysis of the Short Story "Municipality and Stray Dogs". IRJAH, 40: pp. 17-28.

Lashari, M. A. (2013). Jadeed adbi tanqidi nazarya (Sindhi).
Sukkar: My Publication Press.

Lawrence, D.H. (1983). *The White Stocking.* The Prussian officer and Other Stories. Ed. John Worthen. Cambridge UP. Pp. 143-164.

Levi-Strauss, Claude. *Structural Anthropology. (1958).* Mayne, Judith. S/Z and Film Criticism. Jump Cut 12/13 (1976): pp. 41-45.

Lodge, David & Nigel Wood. (1988). *Modern Criticism and Theory.* New York:

Longman.

Lodge, D. (2000). *Modern Criticism and Theory (2nd* ed.). New York: Pearson Education Inc.

Malik, M. A. (2013). *The levels of Power relationship in The Kite Runner.* International Journal of literature, linguistics, and languages.

Malik, W. H., Zaib, S. & Bhugio, F. (2014). *Theory into Practice: An Application of Five Codes Theory on Bina Shah's Short Story, The Optimist,* SAVAP, 5(5): pp. 242-50.

Margaret, Oliphant. (1896). *The Anti-Marriage League',* Blackwood's Magazine. Retrieved from http://www.bl.uk/romantics-and-victorians/articles/an-introduction-tojude-the-obscure#sthash.Ci2vu7EE.dpuf. 18/04/2016.

McFarlane, Brian. Novel to Film: *An Introduction to the Theory of Adaptation.* Oxford: Clarendon Press, 1996.

Meredith, James. (1952). Immanuel Kant The Critique Of

Judgement. London: Oxford University Press.

Mills, M. A., Claus, J. P. & Diamond, S. (Ed.). (2003*). South Asian Folklore: An Encyclopedia*. London: Routledge.

Mikkonen, Kai. (2010). *Remediation and the Sense of Time in Graphic Narratives. In The Rise and Reason of Comics and Graphic Literature*: Critical Essays on the Form, edited by Goggin, Joyce, and Dan Hassler-Forest, 74-86. Jefferson: McFarland & Company.

Moghadam, Farideh Davoodi. (2009). *Methodology of 'Sheikh San'an' in Terms of Binary Oppositions*. Bahar-e-Adab: pp. 63-80.

Moien, M. (1975). *Lexicon Persian* , Tehran. Amir Kabir.

Moriarty, M. (1991). *Roland Barthes*. California: Stanford University Press.

Moshaveri, Zohreh, Mohammad Reza Nasr Esfahani, & Seyed Morteza Hashemi. (2012). Comparative Analysis of 'Sheikh San'an vs Siddhartha. *Comparative Literature*: pp. 241-263.

Mozaffarzad, M. (2013). *Roland Barthes' Narrative Codes in the*

Reading of Sam Shepard's "Buried Child": A Reader-Response Approach, Voices in Asia, 1(1): pp.107-119.

Mulvey, Laura. (1975). *Visual pleasure and narrative cinema. Feminisms: an anthology of literary theory and criticism*: pp. 438-48.

Malik, M. A. (2013). *The levels of Power relationship in The Kite Runner.* International Journal of literature, linguistics, and languages.

Nina, F. (2008). *The Issue of cultural identity in Khaled Hosseini's The Kite Runner.* Jakarta: University Syarif Hidayatullah

Najibi Fini, B. (2006). *Mazandaran and Alborz in Shahnameh.* Pazhuhesh- Nameh Farhang-o-Adab. The second-year No tow.

Naseer, A. (n.d.). *The students' Urdu-English dictionary.* Lahore: Kitab Manzil.

Niaz, A. (2009). *Mirza Ghalib in Yale-Author Sara Suleri Reads From Her New Book*: Boys

Will Be Boys: A Daughter's Elegy, Jazbah Magazine, Women of

Pakistan. Retrieved from http://kazbar.org/jazbah/bookbwb.php 20
March 2016.

Nichols, B. (1985). *Movies and Methods: An anthology*. London:
California University Press.

Nina, F. (2008). *The Issue of cultural identity in Khaled Hosseini's
The Kite Runner.* Jakarta: University Syarif Hidayatullah.

Orr, C. (1984). *The discourse on adaptation.* Wide Angle 6.2: pp.
72-76.Ovid. Metamorphoses.

Peng, Y.-Y. (2018). *Analysis of Hassan's Tragedy in The Kite
Runner from The Three-Dimensional Ethical Perspective.*
Canadian Centre of Science and Education.

Peters, Cleanth. (1971). *Structuration of the Novel-Text: Method &
Analysis. Signs of the
Times: Introductory Readings in Textual Semiotics.* ed. Heath,
Stephen, Colin MacCabe, and Christopher Prendergast.

peng, Y.-Y. (2018). *Analysis of Hassan's Tragedy in The Kite
Runner from The Three-Dimensional Ethical Perspective.*
Canadian Centre of Science and Education.

Pshahil, M. P. (2015). *Colonial Invasion and Inner Conflicts of Afghanistan in Khaled Hosseini's The Kite Runner and A Thousand Splendid Suns.* Robin, J. *Exploring Addolescents.*

Pier, John. (2003). *On the Semiotic Parameters of Narrative:* A Critique of Story and Discourse. What is Narratology?: Questions and Answers Regarding the Status of a Theory. Ed. Tom Kindt and Hans-Harald Müller Berlin: Walter de Gruyter. Pp. 73-98. Plato. Republic.

Pirzaye Khabazi, M. (2014). Iranian flag semiotics based on Shahnameh. Journal of Education and Research. The second-year No Five.

Propp, Vladimir. (1928). *The Morphology of The Folk Tale.* Texas: University of Texas Press.

Propp, Vladmir. (1984). *Theory and History of Folklore. Trans.* Ariadna & Richard Martin. Ed. Anatoly Liberman. Minneapolis: University of Minnesota Press.

Pshahil, M. P. (2015). *Colonial Invasion and Inner Conflicts of Afghanistan in Khaled Hosseini's The Kite Runner and A Thousand Splendid Suns.*

Purwanti, D. (2013). *Five Codes of Roland Barthes in Tennessee Williams' The Glass Menagerie:* A Structuralism Analysis. Retrieved from http://thesis.binus.ac.id/Doc/Lain-lain/2012-2-00450-IG%20WorkingPaper001.pdf January 2, 2016.

Rafat, T.(1985). *Arrival Of The Monsoon, Collected Poems.* Lahore: Vanguard publishers.

Rafat, T. (n.d). Retrieved from https://wikipe.org/wiki/TaufeeqRafaton April 2016.

Rahman, T. (1991). *Work and other short stories.* Lahore: Sang-e-Meel publications.

Raza, A. (2003). *Poetry: Literature Around The World. Lahore*: Ali press.

Ribière, M. (2008). *Barthes: A beginner's guide.* Terrill Hall: Penrith.

Robinson. A. (2011). *An A to Z of Theory | Roland Barthes: Death of the Author*. Retrieved from https://ceasefiremagazine.co.uk/in-theory-barthes-4/ 25/12/2015

Robinson, D.W. (1987). *The Narration of Reading in Joyce's "The Sisters," "An Encounter," and "Araby."* Texas Studies in Literature and Language, 29 (4), 377-396.

Rohani, Masoud, & Ali Akbar Shobklayee. (2012). Analysis of Attar's 'Sheikh San'an' in Terms of Greimas's Actantial Model. *Persian Language and Literature (Gowhar-i-Guya)*: pp. 89-112.

Rosenthal, Peggy. (Oct 1975). *Deciphering S/Z. College English,* 37.2: pp. 124-144.

Sadeghi, L. (2008). *Semiology review cock story Ebrahim Golestan. Tehran.* Neveshta Jornal. No 13.

Saussure, Ferdinand de. 1959. *Course in General Linguistics.* New York: Philosophical Library.

Salah, S. (n.d.). *Spoken Arabic in Saudia Arabia.* Riyadh:

International Public Press.

Saleem, Mohammad. (2013). Investigating Hemingway's Cat in the Rain within the The framework of Barthesian codes. *Interdisciplinary Journal of Contemporary Research in Business*: pp. 106-116.

Sarah, H. *Literary Translation Quality Assesment.* The University of Silesia.

Saussure, Ferdinand de. (1959). *Course in General Linguistics.* New York: Philosophical Library.

Scheiber, Andrew J. (1991). Sign, Seme, and the Psychological Character: Some Thoughts on Roland Barthes' *'S/Z' and the Realistic Novel.* The Journal of Narrative Technique 21.3: pp. 262-273.

Scholes, Robert. (1975). *Structuralism and Literature.* New Haven: Yale University Press.

Scholes, R. (1982). *Semiotics and Interpretation.* New Haven, London: Yale University Press.

Selden, R., Widdowson, R., & Brooker, P. (Eds). (2005). A reader's guide to Contemporary literary theory. 5th ed. London: Pearson Longman.

Shahraz, Q. (2007). *A pair of jeans. In Muneeza Shamsie* (Ed.), And the world changed: Contemporary short stories by Pakistani women. (pp. 157-168). Karachi: Oxford University Press.

Shamsie, M. (2007). *And the world changed:* Contemporary short stories by Pakistani

women. Karachi: Oxford UP.

Siddiqui, M. A. (June 2014). *An interview with Qaisra Shahraz.* ASIATIC 8(1)n.

Smith, Margeret. (1932). *The Persian Mystics: Attar.* New York: E.   P.   Dutton   &
The company, INC.

Soltani, F. (2014). *An Analysis of Sheikh Sanaan's Story Based on Roland Barthes's Theory of codes.* Iran: Sobh-e-Sadegh Institute of Higher Education Isfahan.

Sanders, Julie. (2006). *Adaptation and Appropriation.* New York: Routledge.

Satya, F. H. (2016). *Racial discrimination towards the Hazaras as reflected in Khalid Hosseini's The Kite Runner.* Semarang: Diponegoro University.

Sojoodi, F. (2011). Applied Semitics. Tehran. Elmi.

Sri, U. (2011). *Neo-colonialism in Afghanistan as a representation of America in Khaled Hosseini Novel The Kite Runner.* Semarang: English department Faculty of languages and arts Semarang state university.

Strickland, G. (1983). *Structuralism Or Criticism? Thoughts On How We Read.* Britain: University Press.Cambridge. SEIKO, Concise digital Oxford Dictionary. Thesaurus& Spellchecker.ER6100

Sundaresan Sulekha, D. K. (2017). *Literature Portray of Novel The Kite Runner by Khaled Hosseini.*

Suleri, S. (1991). Meatless Days. Chicago: University of Chicago Press.

Suleri, S. (2003). *Boys Will Be Boys: A Daughter's Elegy*. Illinois: University of Chicago Press.

Tallat, M. and Ghani, M. (2004). *The Metaphor of Meatless Days*. Journal of Research Bahauddin Zakariya University Multan Pakistan, 5: pp. 35-47.

Tallat, M. (2013). *A Style for Reflection*. ELF, Annual Research Journal 15: pp.101-108.

Taghavi, Mohammad. (2010). *From Kaaba to Rome*: Comparative Studies of Sheikh

San'an and Goethe's Faust. *Persian Language and Literature*: pp. 1-28.

Tamara, P. J. (2013). *Amir's Anxiety and Motive in Khaled Hosseini's The Kite Runner*. Semarang: Humanities Dian Nuswantoro University Semarang.

Tarana, D. P. (2015). *The Kite Runner: Role of Multicultural Fiction in Fostering Cultural Competence.* International Journal.

Trimbur, J. (Spring, 2000). *Agency and the Death of the Author:* A Partial Defense of Modernism. Vol. 20, No. 2 Journal of Advanced Composition.

Vanderbeke, Dirk. (2010). *It Was the Best of Two Worlds, It Was the Worst of Two Worlds:* The Adaptation of Novels in Comics and Graphic Novels. In The Rise and Reason of Comics and Graphic Literature: Critical Essays on the Form, edited by Goggin, Joyce, and Dan Hassler-Forest, 104-118. Jefferson: McFarland & Company.

Verde, A., et.al., (2006). *The Narrative Structure of Psychiatric Report. International Journal of Law and Psychiatry,* 29: pp. 1-12.

Vered Tohar, Merva Asef, Anat Kainan, Rakefet Shahar. (2007). *An Alternative Approach for personal Narrative Interpretation:* The Semiotics of Roland Barthes. *International Journal of Qualitative Methods:* pp. 57-70.

Wardrip-Fruin, Noah, and Pat Harrigan. (2004). FirstPerson: New Media as Story, Performance, and Game. MIT Press.

Waugh, P. (2006). *Literary Theory and Criticism: An Oxford Guide*. New York, NY: Oxford University Press.

Willette. J. (2013). *Roland Barthes: "The Death of the Author"*. Retrieved from http://www.arthistoryunstuffed.com/roland-barthes-the-death-of-the-author/ [15/02/2016]

Wilkinson, L.P. (1969) *The Georgics of Virgil: A Critical Study*. Cambridge: Cambridge University Press.

Wilson III & Raymond J. (2008). *A Map of Terms*. The American Journal of Semiotics 15.1/4.

Wolfgang. I. (1972-78). *The Implied Reader: Patterns of Communication in Prose Fiction from Bunyan to Beckett. Baltimore, Maryland*: The Johns Hopkins University Press.

Yaghoobi, Claudia. (2012). *Against the Current: Farid al-Din 'Attar's Diverse Voices."* Persian Literary Studies Journal *(PLSJ)*: pp. 87-109.

Zaib, S. & Mashori, G. M. (2014). *Five Codes of Barthes in Shahraz' Story a Pair of Jeans*: A Post-Structural Approach, ELF, Annual Research Journal, 16: pp. 171-184.

Zamani,Karim . (2006). *A Comprehensive Description of Masnavi* Tehran. Ettelat.

Zanjani, Mahmood. (2001). *Comprehensive Dictionary of Shahnameh*. Tehran. Atayee.

ABOUT THE AUTHOR

Mr. Mubashar Altaf is a lecturer in English at the University of Sargodha, sub-campus Mianwali. He was born in Pakistan on 02 December 1979. He got his MPhil degree in English literature & Linguistics in 2015. He has vast experience in teaching and research. He is a teacher, writer, and critic. He has participated in various research conferences. He has also chaired a session in the first national conference entitled as RCELL conducted by Ali's Theatre, Mandi Bahauddin. He has written five books so far.

Printed in Great Britain
by Amazon

82049221R00130